"Cameron's strong faith comes through in his book and there is no doubt that he was inspired to write it, and I'm sure you'll be inspired after having read it."

—**Lou Holtz**, National Champion and Head Football Coach, *University of Notre Dame*, 1985-1996

"I believe Cameron does a great job of presenting the reader one very necessary yet uncomfortable question: What do you truly believe and live versus what the Gospels have to say? *Twelve Paradoxes of the Gospel* not only uses Scripture, but real life stories to help us answer this question."

—**David Green**, Founder and CEO, *Hobby Lobby*

"I enjoyed the uplifting stories and examples from this truly inspirational book. I will be giving this book to others. Thank you for writing it."

—**Jason Williams**, Cub Scout Committee Chairman, *Boy Scouts of America*

"Thank you for writing such an informative and inspirational book. You have done an excellent job of explaining many of the teachings of the Gospel that can be difficult to understand, or that seem contradictory."

—**Dr. Peter H. Harris**, *Harris Chiropractic & Acupuncture*

"This book was truly a joy to read. It filled me with peace and hope. It left me with a 'fire in the belly' for Christ and a stronger desire to forgive. A must read for everyone!"

—**Melvin Lawson**, General Manager, *Builders FirstSource*

Twelve PARADOXES of the Gospel

CAMERON C. TAYLOR

Published by
Tremendous Life Books
206 West Allen Street
Mechanicsburg, PA 17055

This book is a work of:

Does Your Bag Have Holes? Foundation.
428 E. Thunderbird Road #504, Phoenix, AZ 85022
Phone: 1-877-No-Holes (664-6537) Fax: 1-480-393-4432
CustomerService@DoesYourBagHaveHoles.org
http://www.DoesYourBagHaveHoles.org

ISBN: 978-1-933715-98-8

Printed in the United States of America

To the many who have toiled
and sacrificed to bring the inspired
words of the Bible to the world.

CONTENTS

PREFACE

When my book *Does Your Bag Have Holes?* was first released, I had my staff provide a complimentary copy to each of the postal workers who were shipping orders for the book all across the country. One day I was in the post office mailing some items. When I handed the clerk my credit card to pay, he looked at the name on the card and said, "Hey, you are the author of the book *Does Your Bag Have Holes?*" He then looked at me somewhat perplexed and asked, "Did you really write that book?" I replied, "Yes. I would be considered the author of the book." Having a hard time believing I was the author, he again looked at the name "Cameron C. Taylor" on the credit card and then looked at me and said, "You couldn't have written that book. It is really good." His comment brought a smile to my face, and I said, "I will take that as a great compliment because while I was the one to put words on the page, I give all honor and praise for the book to God. I was merely an instrument in the hands of God." The postal worked then replied, "That makes sense. I knew you had to have help."

Philo T. Farnsworth, the inventor of television, wrote, "I know that God exists. I know that I have never invented anything. I have been a medium by which these things were given to the culture as fast as the culture could earn them. I give all the credit to God."[1] I echo his words. I have never created a book. I give all the credit to God.

Why I Use Different Bible Translations

I have referenced eleven different Bible translations throughout this book. I have done this for two reasons: First, the study of various translations can give further insight to the meaning of the Bible's original text. The original text of the Bible contains

11,280 unique words in Hebrew, Aramaic, and Greek. The English translations of the Bible only contain about 6,000 unique words. For example, in the New Testament there are seven different Greek words with slightly different meanings that are all translated into the single English word "servant." Second, often we think we know what a verse is saying because we have heard it many times. Viewing other translations can help us see a familiar scripture in a new light, revealing a deeper or alternative meaning.

Nondenominational

The teachings throughout this book focus on principles taught and accepted by all Christian denominations—faith, prayer, grace, charity, and so on. All the teachings are founded upon biblical principles, but nothing taught in this book is unique to a particular denomination.

INTRODUCTION

The gospel of Jesus Christ is filled with paradoxes. Many of God's directions appear to be contrary to logic and reason. On the surface they appear to have the opposite effect of the promised result. In this book, we will explore twelve of these gospel paradoxes, taken directly from the Bible.

Since many gospel directives are paradoxical, we must act on faith to live them. God is our Creator and as such is the best source of information on how to ensure our experience on earth is as He intended. God knows how to protect us from harm. God knows how to ensure we perform at our best. God knows how to help us reach our full potential. Many items we purchase come with an instruction manual from its creator on how to ensure the items work properly. God has given us the Bible as the owner's manual for our protection, maintenance, and growth. If we believe God is our Creator, then we should also believe that His words are the best source for our correct operation.

"Trust in the Lord with all thine heart; and lean not unto thine own understanding. In all thy ways acknowledge him, and he shall direct thy paths."
—Proverbs 3:5–6, King James Version

CHAPTER 1

THE PARADOX OF FAITH

"He that findeth his life shall lose it: and he that loseth his life for my sake shall find it."
—Matthew 10:39, King James Version

A church leader taught, "One of life's paradoxes is that a person who approaches everything with a what's-in-it-for-me attitude may acquire money, property, and land, but in the end will lose the fulfillment and the happiness that a person enjoys who shares his talents and gifts generously with others."

Abraham Maslow created a theory on how people fulfill their needs. Maslow's hierarchy of needs is represented as a pyramid, with the larger lower levels representing the basic needs of food, air, water, and shelter, and the upper point representing the need to seek a power greater than oneself and to serve others. One of the fundamental ideas is that there is a specific order in which we seek to fulfill our needs. For example, Maslow's hierarchy teaches that we must fulfill our need for food before we seek to fulfill our need for security, and that we must fill our need for security before we can seek a power greater than ourselves.

Jesus Christ taught us a different way to fulfill our needs. His teachings are completely contrary to the ideas of Maslow. Christ taught in Matthew 6:33, "But seek ye first the kingdom of God, and his righteousness; and all these things shall be added unto you." While Maslow's theory explains how people driven by fear and selfishness seek to fulfill needs, it does not describe how people of faith seek to fulfill needs. People of faith seek God before food, security, or friends. People of faith know that by seeking the will of God first, all their needs will be fulfilled.

Principle of Indirection

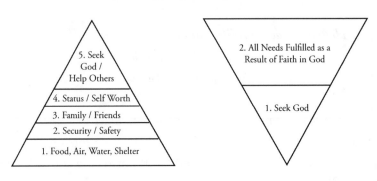

Fear Driven / Selfish   *Faith Driven / Selfless*

Parable of the Stationary Bike

Trying to satisfy our human needs without faith in God is like trying to win the Tour de France on a stationary exercise bike. You can pedal as long and hard as those on a racing bike, but at the end of the race you will still be in the same place. The person on the stationary bike can pedal, work, and sweat, but will get nowhere. Truly fulfilling human needs requires application of the principle of indirection. We can't satisfy our human needs by directly seeking them. Instead we must first seek God and serve others. The Savior taught, "He that findeth his life shall lose it; and he that loseth his life for my sake shall find it."[1]

The indirect approach of seeking God is the first step to truly satisfying our needs. Those who are driven by fear and selfishness will attempt to satisfy their needs first, but will find it impossible to truly fulfill their needs.

PARABLE OF THE STATIONARY BIKE™
Put God Last ... Go Nowhere Fast

The more you make the fulfillment of your needs your target, the more you will miss it. True fulfillment of your needs cannot be obtained by direct pursuit. True fulfillment of your needs will come as a result of your personal dedication to God and service to others. If you put God last, you will go nowhere fast.

Parable of Heaven and Hell

A noble Chinese warrior died in battle and arrived at the heavenly portals. He requested that he be allowed to see what hell was like before entering heaven. His request was granted. Much to his surprise, he was taken to a magnificent chamber. In this chamber, there were tables heaped with an abundance of the most desirable foods one could imagine. However, the people in the room were cursing and screaming in anger. The warrior was initially puzzled at their behavior, but he soon understood their plight. They were trying to eat with chopsticks that were three feet long. They could pick up their food, but because their chopsticks were so long, it was impossible to place the food in their mouths. To his surprise, when the warrior entered heaven he saw a similar scene. He once again saw a magnificent chamber filled with tables of delicious food, and the guests at the table had the same chopsticks that were three feet long. This room, however, was not filled with frustration, anger, and cursing. It was instead filled with sounds of laughter and joy. The difference was that those in heaven had learned to feed one another. In giving, they received.

PARABLE OF HEAVEN AND HELL

Heaven

Hell

As we lose our lives in the service of others, we find our true selves and experience the miracle of the paradox of faith.

Parable of the Baseball Bat

Let's say a Major League Baseball player hits seventy-four home runs in a season and breaks the single-season home-run record.

Does the bat receive the credit? Is the bat somehow better than the other bats and thus entitled to recognition? In the record book, is partial credit given to the bat? Of course not. The bat hits home runs because of the batter. In our relationship with God, we can be compared to a baseball bat. We can do nothing by ourselves. How many home runs would a bat hit if it were to enter the batter's box alone? The bat is going to lie in the dirt and do nothing. The bat can do nothing by itself, just as we can do nothing by ourselves.

With God

Without God

If a home run is hit, does the crowd honor the bat because it actually made contact with the ball and hit it out of the park? Of course not. However, often in our lives we take credit for our accomplishments or honor others' accomplishments with little or no credit given to God. When people take credit for their accomplishments, it is as foolish as giving praise to a baseball bat for hitting a home run. When we understand our true relationship with God, we realize He is the source of all our accomplishments and abilities.

The Savior teaches this principle in John 15:4–5: "As the branch cannot bear fruit of itself, except it abide in the vine; no more can ye, except ye abide in me. I am the vine, ye are the branches: He that abideth in me, and I in him, the same bringeth forth much fruit: for without me ye can do nothing."

"Christ does not say, without me ye can do but little, neither does He say, without me ye cannot do any [difficult] thing; nor without me ye can do it with difficulty: But He says, without me ye can do nothing!"[2]

In order to hit a home run, both a batter and a bat are required. This is where we come in. We must allow Christ to utilize us as instruments in His hands. Our role in bringing to pass righteousness and achieving greatness is submitting to His will. Our role is to become instruments in the Master's hands.

Thy Will Be Done

Once we forget our will and desires and submit to the will and desire of the Lord, we can truly become great. As C. S. Lewis taught, "Give up yourself, and you will find your real self. Lose your life and you will save it. Submit to death, death of your ambitions and favorite wishes every day and death of your whole body in the end: submit with every fiber of your being, and you will find eternal life. Keep back nothing. Nothing that you have not given away will ever be really yours. Nothing in you that has not died will ever be raised from the dead. Look for yourself, and you will find in the long run only hatred, loneliness, despair, rage, ruin, and decay. But look for Christ and you will find Him, and with Him everything else thrown in."[3]

You may now ask, if we all are doing the will of God, are we not all exactly the same? No. Actually, coming to Christ and turning our life over to Him cultivates diversity. As we come to Christ we find our true selves. We come to see how different we truly are. Let's take power tools, for example. There are all kinds of power tools—drills, sanders, saws, and so forth. They are all tools, but each is very different. The difference between these tools is manifest when they are plugged into an outlet—the tools' power source. When the tools are operating on electricity they demonstrate how different they are. The sander smoothes objects, the drill produces holes, and the saw cuts. Each is operating on the same power source, but each is very different. Many seek an alternative power source. They try to operate according to their wills and desires. As we strive to resist Christ and live on our own, the more dominated we become by our environment, upbringing, and natural desires. What we call "my desires" simply become the desire of the flesh—the desires of a natural person. As people submit to what they call "desires," they become much the same as the thousands of natural people who sought to fulfill their wills and desires. "Sameness is to be found most among the most 'natural' men, not among those who surrender to Christ. How monotonously alike all the great tyrants and conquerors have been: how glorious different are the saints. . . . The more we get what we 'now call ourselves' out of the way and let Him take over, the more truly ourselves we become."[4]

Walking on Water

As I was researching the topic of faith, several times I came across the story of Jesus walking on the water. The story reads, "Jesus went unto them, walking on the sea. And when the disciples saw him walking on the sea, they were troubled, saying, It is a spirit; and they cried out for fear. But straightway Jesus spake unto them, saying, Be of good cheer; it is I; be not afraid. And Peter answered him and said, Lord, if it be thou, bid me come unto thee on the water. And he said, Come. And when Peter was come down out of the ship, he walked on the water, to go to Jesus. But when he saw the wind boisterous, he was afraid; and beginning to sink, he cried, saying, Lord, save me. And immediately Jesus stretched forth his hand, and caught him, and said unto him, O thou of little faith, wherefore didst thou doubt?"[5]

I read through numerous commentaries on these verses, talking about Peter's doubt and fear that caused him to sink. As I pondered the verses, I continually felt that I was missing some key lessons that were to be learned from this story. I began to wonder why Peter would ask to come out onto the water when Jesus was coming to get into the boat. After many hours of pondering, the spiritual impression came to me that Jesus had been teaching and telling the apostles that they were to do all the miracles that they had seen Him do. Matthew 10:5–8 reads, "These twelve Jesus sent forth, and commanded them, saying . . . Heal the sick, cleanse the lepers, raise the dead, cast out devils: freely ye have received, freely give." They were to do many mighty miracles as they had seen the Savior do. He told them that with faith they would be able to perform miracles and that nothing would be impossible to them.

When Peter saw Christ walking on the water, he had faith that if Jesus could walk on water so could he. For Christ had not only told Peter that through faith he could perform miracles but had also commanded Peter to perform miracles in His name. So Peter, seeing the miracle of walking on water, exercised his faith to perform this miracle also. A key to understanding this story is the phrase, "when Peter was come down out of the ship, he walked on the water."[6] Peter walked on water. It is not surprising that Jesus walked on water. He is God. He fed five thousand with two fish and five loaves of bread, He cast out devils, He raised the dead, and He healed the sick. I believe it is much easier to believe that Christ can perform such miracles than it is to believe that we can perform such miracles in His name. The most amazing part of the story is that Peter, a mere man, walked on water. I wondered why Jesus would have answered, "Come," in response to Peter's request to walk on the water. What was the purpose? The impression that came to me in answer to this question was that Jesus was showing Peter, the other disciples in the boat, and each of us who reads the New Testament today that with faith in Christ we can each do the mighty miracles that Christ performed. Reading about Peter walking on water should increase our faith to perform miracles in the name of the Lord. If we believe in Christ, signs and miracles will occur. Mark 16:17–18 reads, "And these signs shall follow them that believe; In my name shall they cast out devils; they shall speak with new tongues; they shall take up serpents; and if they drink any deadly thing, it shall not hurt them: they shall lay hands on the sick, and they shall recover."

Jesus is saying to each of us, "If thou canst believe, all things are possible."[7] We should each strive to follow the example of the disciple Stephen found in Acts 6:8: "And Stephen, full of faith and power, did great wonders and miracles among the people."

Modern-Day Miracle

I completed writing about Peter walking on water right before I left for a weeklong summer camp with the young men in our congregation. On Tuesday I shared with the young men in our campsite the story of Jesus and Peter walking on the water and told them that they each had the power and had been directed by Christ to perform miracles in His name. On Wednesday morning, one of the leaders, Scott Lewis, from a neighboring campsite, stopped by our campsite and asked for a blessing of healing. Scott had a severe case of food poisoning. I asked Scott to say a prayer before the blessing, and then Preston Dixon anointed his head with oil and I sealed the anointing and gave him a blessing. The blessing said he would be healed quickly. I ran into Scott about thirty minutes after the blessing and asked him how he was doing. He said he was still not feeling well. Since the blessing said he would be healed quickly, I expected him to be feeling better. I then had the impression that I needed to get everyone in our summer camp to pray that Scott Lewis would be healed.

Everyone was then gathering for breakfast at our central dining area, so I grabbed my scriptures and went over to the dining area. I asked for everyone's attention and told them that their help was needed. I then read to them James 5:14–16: "Is any sick among you? Let him call for the elders of the church; and let them pray over him, anointing him with oil in the name of the Lord: And the prayer of faith shall save the sick, and the Lord shall raise him up . . . and pray one for another, that ye may be healed. The effectual fervent prayer of a righteous man availeth much." I told all those at breakfast that we had anointed Scott with oil and had provided a blessing of healing, but that their faith and prayers were needed. I asked each of them to offer a prayer that Scott Lewis would be healed.

I asked Brother Scott Lewis to write down the experience. He recorded the following:

> On Wednesday morning a little before dawn I woke up with a nauseating feeling in my stomach. I started going up to the outhouse every 5–10 minutes with bouts of diarrhea. After the first hour, I had progressed from mere diarrhea to heavy vomiting and constant diarrhea. To make things worse, I knew I was getting dehydrated, which would lead to far worse problems. I was unable to hold water down and had a deep dread that I was in serious trouble. My mind raced thinking of potential ways to shake the bug. I couldn't hold down water, food was out of the question, and I couldn't lie down and get some rest. I was going back and forth to the outhouse and sometimes making it all the way, other times not. I was in deep trouble and knew it.
>
> I began wandering from site to site looking for an Elder that had some oil so I could receive a blessing. Unfortunately, the first few people I asked were like me, packing everything we thought we needed and forgetting the one thing that would help to bring the power of God to bear. Luckily a few brethren from another campsite had some oil. As soon as they answered in the affirmative, I asked for a blessing of healing.
>
> The blessing started as most blessings do. I listened and expected to hear that I would be healed

over time and would return to normal. I had a feeling I would need to be rushed home quickly and probably need hospitalization. The dehydration was bad enough that I felt lightheaded, dry-mouthed, and chilled. As the blessing continued, the words were mouthed, "You will be healed quickly and completely." This shook me a bit. I had great desires to stay at the camp and enjoy time with the young men, but I had feared that I needed to leave promptly. The blessing was closed, and I sat for just a moment in awe. I thanked the brethren and hoped that it would indeed be fulfilled. As soon as I got back to camp, the dehydration hit me. I had to scurry back up to the now well-used facilities to expel more water and lightheadedly walked back to camp. Cameron (one of the two men who had given me the blessing) asked me as I passed how I was doing. I replied that I wasn't doing too much better, but that I was comforted by the blessing.

I returned to camp and collapsed into a folding chair. My neck seemed to have no strength, and it bobbed a bit and I just let it hang. I heard the boys getting up and going to breakfast. I said hello and smiled as best I could as they left for breakfast. I was so lightheaded that I kept passing out, and I was feeling as close to death as I have ever felt. My body was absolutely drained and my spirit was weak. It was around this time that I heard from the dining area Cameron speaking to the boys. I perked up my ears and heard him read a scripture about faith and healing. I didn't catch it all, but at the end I heard "the prayer of a righteous man availeth much." After that he asked that they take a moment to pray for sick brother Lewis. Silence stretched for about 30 seconds. Then, almost like a sudden gust of wind I felt infused with energy. I felt the power of God fill my body. I stood right up, walked to the dining area and drank some water, and began prepping for my next class I had to teach. From that moment on, I neither had to vomit or run to the restroom for diarrhea. I finished up the week, enjoying my time teaching and talking with the young men. The blessing had been completely fulfilled. I have no doubt that my own faith was not enough to bring about the miracle of healing. I was down and out and felt beaten. I have full confidence that the faith of those young men and leaders healed me.

Conclusion

Faith is a source of power and strength. Faith is to human life what gasoline is to a chainsaw. Gas is the power source for a chainsaw, which makes it productive and useful. Faith is the fuel that powers the human engine. Faith in Christ gives us power to do things beyond our physical ability and to do things not possible for man alone. Faith allows us to tap into God's power and perform miracles in our lives and the lives of others. With faith you can move mountains, heal the sick, do "great wonders and miracles,"[8] and "nothing will be impossible unto you."[9]

CHAPTER 2

THE PARADOX OF GRACE

*"And he [Christ] said unto me [Paul], My grace is suffi-
cient for thee: for my strength is made perfect in weakness.
Most gladly therefore will I rather glory in my infirmities,
that the power of Christ may rest upon me . . . for when I
am weak, then am I strong."*
—2 Corinthians 12:9–10, King James Version

"This is the paradox of grace. He who insists he is right will be
pronounced wrong, while he who admits he is wrong will be
declared right."[1]

The Lord taught this principle in the parable of the Pharisee
and the Publican, saying, "Two men went up into the temple to
pray; the one a Pharisee, and the other a publican. The Pharisee
stood and prayed thus with himself, God, I thank thee, that I am
not as other men are, extortioners, unjust, adulterers, or even as
this publican. I fast twice in the week, I give tithes of all that I
possess. And the publican, standing afar off, would not lift up so
much as his eyes unto heaven, but smote upon his breast, saying,
God be merciful to me a sinner. I tell you, this man went down
to his house justified rather than the other: for every one that
exalteth himself shall be abased; and he that humbleth himself
shall be exalted."[2]

Grace and the Scratched Ferrari

For several years I volunteered as the scoutmaster in our local troop. Our troop was creating a movie to earn the cinematography merit badge, and we needed to film one of the scenes with a luxury car. One of my neighbors at the time had two beautiful Ferraris, so I arranged with him to film the scene at his home.

My son Mitchell, who was five at the time, came with me for the filming and was to have a part in the scene as an elf. We were in my neighbor's garage, and he was showing me the pictures on his "wall of fame and shame [crashes]" of his various vehicles. As we were looking at the pictures, we heard a crash and turned around to see a chair on the hood of the red Ferrari. In front of the Ferrari was a raised workbench area with a chair on wheels. My son had accidentally knocked the chair off the workbench platform onto the hood of the Ferrari.

My son ran and hid behind one of our friends who was with us, who later told me my son's heart was beating extremely fast as he waited to see what would happen next. We were each in silence looking at my neighbor, and I was quite impressed by his reaction. He remained calm and said to my son, "That is why they make paint; I will be able to have it fixed." To see that his immediate reaction was one of patience, love, and concern for my son illustrated that my neighbor truly was a man who had the attributes of forgiveness, love, and patience.

When we arrived home after filming, I told Mitchell that even though it was an accident, he was still responsible for the damage that he had caused, and he needed to give all his money to our neighbor to help pay for the repair. I returned to my neighbor's home, and I explained my desire to pay to have the Ferrari repaired. I handed him the envelope and told him that my son had emptied his savings and that I had also enclosed a blank check to cover the cost to repair the damage. My neighbor handed me back the envelope and said, "You are a man of honor, but I can't take this." I replied, "I am responsible for the damage, and I want to pay to fix it. It's not fair for you to be responsible for it." My neighbor then explained that he would be able to have it repaired, and that I did not need to worry about it. He then said, "I view it as a gift."

My neighbor extended forgiveness and grace to me and my son. He agreed as a gift to pay for the damage to his Ferrari that we were responsible for. Likewise, Christ has paid the price for our sins so we do not have to.

We each sin and as a result are in a fallen and imperfect state that separates us from God. Romans 3:23 states, "For all have sinned, and come short of the glory of God." There is no way for us to perfect ourselves, so a Savior was provided to save us from our sins. Only through Christ's grace can we be forgiven and avoid paying the penalty for our sins. The New Testament records, "And being in an agony [Christ] prayed more earnestly: and his sweat was as it were great drops of blood falling down to the ground."[3] Christ has paid to repair the damage each time we metaphorically scratch a Ferrari with sin.

Just as my neighbor lifted the burden of payment for the damage to the Ferrari, so has Christ lifted from us the burden of sin through his atoning sacrifice in the garden of Gethsemane and on the cross. The book of Romans declares, "While we were yet sinners, Christ died for us. . . . Being now justified by his blood, we shall be saved from wrath through him. . . . Being reconciled, we shall be saved by his life. And . . . we also joy in God through our Lord Jesus Christ, by whom we have now received the atonement. Wherefore, as by one man [Adam] sin entered into the world, and death by sin; and so death passed upon all men, for . . . all have sinned. . . . For . . . the grace of God, and the gift by grace . . . hath abounded unto many . . . the free gift

. . . of . . . justification . . . the gift of righteousness shall reign in life by one, Jesus Christ. . . . For as by one man's [Adam's] disobedience many were made sinners, so by the obedience of one [Christ] shall many be made righteous. . . . As sin hath reigned unto death, even so might grace reign through righteousness unto eternal life by Jesus Christ our Lord."[4]

The Parable of the Pit

Let's say you have fallen down a mile-deep pit. You try to climb the walls, but it's impossible. The walls of the pit go straight up, and there is nothing to hold onto. Each attempt you make to climb the wall has the same result. You end up falling back to the bottom of the pit.

As a result of the fall of Adam, we have all sinned and thus fall short of the perfection required to be in the presence of God. Spiritually you have fallen into a mile-deep pit. You try as hard as you can to overcome your fallen nature, for you want to get right with God. You try to keep all the commandments, but you fail. So you try to do a lot of good works hoping that maybe they will sway the judgment of God in your favor. You hope that somehow if your good works outweigh your sins, you can get right with God. However, even after all your good works you still are far from perfect and thus unable to escape the pit. You now begin to realize that it's impossible to get yourself out of this spiritual pit and fall into despair because you want so badly to escape. All of this trying leads you to a vital moment at which you turn to God and say as did the publican, "God be merciful to me a sinner."[5] You are changed from being confident about your own efforts to the state in which you leave it to God and recognize your total dependence upon Him.

At this point, Jesus Christ appears in the pit and declares,

"'Come unto me, all ye that labour and are heavy laden, and I will give you rest. Take my yoke upon you . . . and ye shall find rest unto your souls. For my yoke is easy, and my burden is light.'[6] Come unto me and be saved."

In response to the Master's invitation, you yoke yourself with Him and climb onto His back, and in an instant you are free from the pit. Becoming one with Christ and being freed from the pit of sin is the beginning of your life as a Christian and is the process of justification.

Justification

"As husband and wife become one with each other through the covenant of marriage, so the Savior and the saved become one with each other through the covenant of the gospel. Just as a bride renounces all competing claims upon her loyalties and normally takes her husband's name, so those who enter this covenant with Christ renounce all competing loyalties, put Him first, and take His name upon them. To this union, we bring our righteous desires and our loyalty. He brings His perfection. In the covenant union, what is mine becomes His, and what is His becomes mine. Thus my sins become His for payment, and His righteousness becomes mine for justification. When we become one with Jesus Christ, spiritually we form a partnership with a joint account, and His assets and our liabilities flow into each other. Since He has more assets than we have liabilities, the new account has a positive balance as soon as it is formed, and the partnership is justified, even though its junior partners (you and me) could not make it on their own. This is what the Apostle Paul refers to as being 'in Christ.'"[7]

As a result of the gospel covenant, we are judged according to Christ's merits. We know Christ is perfect and holy without spot, so as we are judged by His merits, we can rest assured that we are in a saved condition before the Father. As a result of this new relationship we are justified and freed from the pit of sin. Justification doesn't mean that you and I suddenly become perfectly obedient and stop sinning. The sinner is declared righteous and perfect not because he or she is perfect, but because he or she is one with Christ and He is righteous and perfect.

The requirement to be justified in Christ is not obedience but a true and sincere desire to become such through Christ. Justification requires that we recognize Christ as our only way out of the pit and that we want Him to take us to perfection and eternal life. Christ does not say, "Climb as far as you can and then I will take you the rest of the way." He says, "Climb on my back, and I will free you from the pit of sin." Christ says, "Come unto me and be saved." To enter the covenant relationship with Christ requires our heart. Justification requires that we want Christ to give us eternal life, that we want to do what Christ asks of us.

Having this desire is referred to in the Bible as being born again. Christ declares, "Verily, verily, I say unto thee, Except a man be born again, he cannot see the kingdom of God."[8] The following analogy can be helpful in determining if you have been born again. A man comes up to you holding a board with two buttons on it. If you push the one, you will never sin again. If you push the other, you can continue to sin. Which button would you push? If you would push the button that would result in your never sinning again, you have illustrated that you don't want to sin even though you do. If you would push the button that would allow you to continue to sin, you have not truly been born again. But being born again does not mean we never sin.

Why do we commit sins even though we have been born

again and justified? We commit sin because of the flesh. The Bible teaches, "For the flesh lusteth against the Spirit, and the Spirit against the flesh: and these are contrary the one to the other: so that ye cannot do the things that ye would."[9] The apostle Paul desired to do righteousness, but because of the flesh he did things he didn't want to do, causing him to exclaim, "For we know that the law is spiritual: but I am carnal, sold under sin. For that which I do I allow not: for what I would, that do I not; but what I hate, that do I . . . . For the good that I would I do not: but the evil which I would not, that I do. . . . O wretched man that I am! Who shall deliver me from the body of this death?"[10]

Was Paul breaking his gospel covenants because he sinned? Of course not. Everyone after they enter the covenant of the gospel continues to sin, even though they desire not to sin. A characteristic of one who is in a covenant relationship with Christ is not one who does not sin, but one who fights against and hates sin, as did Paul.

Complete obedience is not required to enter the gospel covenant, but is it required to stay in the covenant? No. It could not be, or we would never be in a covenant relationship with Christ because we continually sin. Through justification we are instantly perfect in Christ, but the gap between our actual performance and personal perfection remains. For obedience to be a requirement to be in a covenant relationship with Christ would mean we would have to be perfect before we could be justified, which defeats the entire purpose of justification. This would be the equivalent of saying, "I know you are in a mile-deep pit, that is impossible for you to get out of by yourself, but I can't help you until you can get yourself out of the pit. As soon as you can get out of the pit, I will come into the pit and take you to safety." God does not justify the righteous but the ungodly.[11] Christ declares, "They that are whole have no need of the physician, but they that are sick: I came not to call the righteous, but sinners to repentance."[12]

Sanctification

Once we have experienced the instantaneous gift of justification, we then begin the process of sanctification. "Justification and sanctification both come by God's gracious will. Yet they are different things. Justification is a single act whereby God graciously declares the ungodly person not guilty. Sanctification is a continual process whereby God graciously changes a believer's habits and behavior into holy deeds. . . . The former is instantaneous; the latter is progressive. The persons on whom the blessing of sanctification is bestowed are those who are justified. Holiness is a wonderful blessing of the new covenant, not a condition to our entry into that covenant."[13]

As we enter a covenant relationship with Christ, we place our faith in Christ to save us. Thus, we will want to do the things He asks us to do. Some have foolishly declared, "'Faith is all that matters. Consequently, if you have faith, it doesn't matter what you do. Sin away, my lad, and have a good time and Christ will see that it makes no difference in the end.' The answer to that nonsense is that, if what you call your 'faith' in Christ does not involve taking the slightest notice of what He says, then it is not Faith at all."[14] The apostle James declared, "I will shew thee my faith by my works."[15] And the apostle Paul taught, "What then? shall we sin, because we are not under the law, but under grace? God forbid."[16] If we believe God is our creator and place our faith in Him, then we will also believe that His words are the best source for directing our life.

The true doctrine of justification by grace does not lead to moral irresponsibility, laziness, passivity, or disobedience. True justification will never lead a person to more sin, but rather will lead to fuller repentance and obedience. If you do not desire obedience (notice I said "desire," not that you are actually obedient), you have not truly entered the covenant that justifies. Sanctification is then the process of aligning our actions with our desire for obedience.

We obtain sanctification by repenting. It is the process of moving to a higher and higher level of obedience. Repentance is the process by which we improve and become more like Christ. Repentance is not an act of going from being a sinner to becoming perfectly obedient. We will not obtain perfect obedience in this life; thus, we are always battling to overcome disobedience. Repentance just lessens the level of disobedience. The process of seeking to become more like Christ is what the scriptures refer to as enduring to the end. Matthew 24:13 declares, "He that shall endure unto the end, the same shall be saved."

What does it mean to endure to the end? Well, what is the end we are seeking? The end we desire is perfection and eternal life. Often the scriptural use of the word "endure" means to continue rather than to suffer. Thus, enduring to the end can be understood to mean continuing toward perfection as we seek to fulfill the command to "Be ye therefore perfect, even as your Father which is in heaven is perfect."[17]

The journey of striving to become like Christ will last a lifetime. Every day God wants you to become a little more like him. Colossians 3:10 declares, "You have begun to live the new life, in which you are being made new and are becoming like the One who made you."[18] Some may seek a way to possess instantly all the attributes of Godliness, but growth is a process. Growth is gradual. The

Bible says, "Our lives gradually becoming brighter and more beautiful as God enters our lives and we become like him."[19]

Obtaining complete obedience through Christ (sanctification) is a long process. There are no shortcuts. Eventually, "We shall become mature people, reaching to the very height of Christ's full stature."[20]

Am I Going to Heaven?

For the past several years, I have been asking Christians in the various classes and seminars I teach to answer the following two questions. "Do you want to go to heaven?" and "If you were to die today, would you go to heaven?" Everyone answers "yes" to the first question, while many answer "no" to the second question. However, the answer to the second question was not as important as why they gave their answer. I asked people to explain why they answered "yes" or "no" to the question, "If you were to die today, would you go to heaven?" The answers of both those who answered "yes" and those who answered "no" revealed that they did not have an understanding, or had a misunderstanding, of how one gains eternal life. The criteria they were using to determine if they were going to heaven was wrong.

Many who answered "no" explained that they were not yet living all the commandments, so they would not qualify for heaven. They felt they were not worthy. Those who answered "yes" gave such answers as "I am living a good life," or "I have not done anything bad this week." The criteria many of the people were using to determine if they were going to heaven was "Am I worthy to go to heaven?" With this criteria, we would all be unworthy to enter heaven. Perfection is the requirement for heaven. We all have sinned and will continue to sin; therefore, we are imperfect, and thus none of us are worthy to go.

To determine if we are going to heaven we must ask, "Am I justified through Christ?" not "Am I worthy?" We are saved by Christ's merits, mercy, and grace through justification. To be justified requires that we enter a covenant relationship with Christ, desire to do what is right, and then try to do what is right. If you can say I have been justified, I want to do what is right, and I try to do what is right, you are in a saved condition. If you were to die, you would go to heaven. Misconceptions about how one obtains heaven have caused many to lose hope or to be filled with unnecessary anxiety concerning their salvation.

Unjustification

Is it possible once justified to move to an unjustified state? Yes, but it is because of a change of desire, not because of sin. Once we have been born again and desire to be obedient to God, that desire must continue in us if we are to remain justified.

We do have to endure to the end, for Christ will not save us if we do not want to be saved. Thus, at any point we could end our covenant relationship and jump off Christ's back and fall back into the pit of sin. Only we can end the covenant relationship with Christ by deciding we no longer want to be righteous and no longer want eternal life—by deciding to stop our fight against sin, and beginning to living in harmony with our sins. Christ will never leave us. When in a covenant relationship with Christ, we do not have to succeed in our fight against sin, but we do have to be fighting. The old saying is true: "A failure is not one who fails, but rather one who fails and then gives up." All who continue in the fight against sin and try to do what God commands will receive perfection and eternal life because that is what God has promised. In the pursuit of perfection and eternal life, there are no losers, only quitters.

Saved by Grace

*"By grace are ye saved through faith; and that not of yourselves; it
is the gift of God; Not of works, lest any man should boast."*
—Ephesians 2:8–9

We can do nothing to earn grace. Grace is the opposite of works
and worthiness. If we deserved to be saved, that would be called
justice, not grace. Grace means undeserved kindness, or favor
given without it being earned in any way. There is nothing we
can do to earn grace, and Christ via His grace does 100 percent
of the saving. Christ has satisfied the demands of justice in the
garden of Gethsemane and on the cross that He may show us
mercy. Until we realize that Christ does 100 percent of the saving, we will never be in the right relationship with Him. We do
not and cannot earn eternal life. It comes as a gift from Christ
through His grace.

The doctrine of salvation by grace does not eliminate the
need for works and obedience but puts them in their proper
place. So if works and obedience don't earn us or make us worthy of salvation, then what role do they play? They enable us to
receive God's grace. For years theologians have argued over
whether we are saved by faith or by works. I will end the argument once and for all. We are not saved by either. We are saved
by Christ and by His grace alone. Our faith and our works do
not save us, but they do allow Christ to save us.

Scissors Analogy

C. S. Lewis uses the analogy of scissors to describe the relationship
between faith and works. He states that both are needed to complete the work of salvation as are two blades of a pair of scissors

needed to complete the task of cutting paper. I believe his analogy could stand a bit of an adjustment. Our faith and our works do not save us because Christ does that. However, our faith and our works do play an essential role. Our faith and our works enable Christ to save us. To adjust the analogy of C. S. Lewis, I would say that Christ represents the two blades of a pair of scissors and that our faith in Christ and our works are the screw that holds the blades together and enables them to function. Thus, our faith and works do not save us, but they enable Christ to save us. As with scissors, the blades do the actual cutting, but the screw enables the cutting to occur. Without the screw holding the blades together, the blades are ineffective in cutting paper. In the work of salvation, Christ can't save us without our enabling faith and works. Why can't Christ save us independent of our faith and works? Because it violates the law of free will and choice. We have to want Him to save us, and want to become like Him, and this is where our faith and works come in.

Corvette Analogy

Some argued that faith and obedience are not required to obtain God's grace—that for it to be grace you have to do absolutely nothing. This argument can be discounted with the following story: Let's say a friend calls you up and tells you he has gift for you—a brand-new Corvette. All you have to do is come and pick it up, and it is yours. Would the fact that you had to pick up the car make it any less of a gift? Would you argue that after you went to your friend's house that he then owed you the car because you earned it by following his condition that you must pick it up? Does going to pick up the car change it from a gift to a wage? Of course not. Your friend asking you to come pick up the car is a way for him to be sure you want the car. If you don't want the car, you don't have to go and get it. In much the same way, God offers us eternal life by His grace as a gift. The offer of eternal life is on the table. We simply have to come and pick it up by having faith in Christ, and if we truly have faith in Christ, we will strive to be obedient to the things He asks us to do.

Seed Analogy

If you have to endure to the end to be saved, don't my works (obedience and repenting) result in my earning eternal life? No. For example, let's say Jimmy wants to grow a garden. However, Jimmy knows nothing about planting or how things grow. Then a master gardener approaches Jimmy and offers to help him grow a garden. Jimmy recognizes him as a master gardener, so he is confident that if he follows the direction given him by the gardener the garden will grow. Jimmy becomes excited to grow a garden and follows all the directions the master gardener gives him. He plants the seeds, waters them, fertilizes them, and weeds the garden, and as a result the garden begins to grow. Jimmy becomes ecstatic that he grew a garden and begins telling everyone about the garden he grew. Jimmy begins to take credit for something he didn't really do. Although Jimmy's planting, watering, and fertilizing are essential for enabling the plants to grow, these actions did not actually make the plants grow. If Jimmy had power to make things grow by planting, watering, and fertilizing, let him plant a rock and make it grow. Jimmy has no more power to make a seed grow then he does to make a rock grow. The growth of the plants comes from God. Just as the natural consequence of planting and watering a plant is that it will grow, so also the natural consequence of obeying God's directives is that we will develop the attributes of Godliness. We can take no credit for becoming more Christlike just as Jimmy can take no credit for growing a garden. Our growth through the process of sanctification comes from Christ.

Being Born Again

The following is extremely personal, but I share it because I believe others may have had or are experiencing something similar. Hopefully, it will help you better understand justification, sanctification, and sin. I was raised in a Christian home, but I didn't really believe what I had been taught. I became involved in immorality, lying, stealing, gambling, and other sins. There was even a point when I denied the existence of God and Christ and declared myself an atheist. Out of high school, I was accepted to a small out-of-state junior college. All of my family had attended a private Christian school and wanted me to do the same, but the Christian school had many rules that would not coincide with the life of sin I had chosen. I chose to live a life of stealing, gambling, and immorality because of the worldly possessions and physical pleasures the sins provided. To refer back to the man with the two buttons analogy, if a man had come to me after high school graduation and held out these two buttons, I would have pushed the button to continue in my sins. I didn't want to quit them. I was addicted to and loved sin. I chose to sin even though I knew it was wrong.

Following my freshman year of college, I had a profound spiritual experience. Our family was traveling to Arizona for vacation, and I was riding in the back seat of my brother's car. My brother was listening to dramatized audiotapes of the New Testament. I later found out what I was listening to was the reading of the Sermon on the Mount. As I listened to Christ's words, I had a spectacular feeling come over me. It felt as though something had entered my body. It is hard to describe, but it was a tingling, warm, peaceful feeling. I knew it was from God, and I could feel it through my entire body, from my head to my toes. Tears began to pour down my face. I knew that what was being said on the tape was true. What I felt was so powerful and convincing that I don't think I would have been any more persuaded had an angel appeared to me. I then had thoughts enter into my mind. One thought was that Jesus does live. It was as clear as if an angel had spoken to me. I then knew that there was a God and that Jesus Christ did live and was the Son of God. Now I could never deny the existence of God and Christ, for these things had been made known unto me by the power of God.

Not only did I come to know that Christ lived, I experienced a change in the way I thought. I was born again. I had a change of heart. I no longer wanted to sin. At this moment, if the man with the two buttons would have come to me, I would have chosen with no reservation the button that would result in my never committing sin again. I wanted to do what was right. Once my desires changed, I was no longer in rebellion with God. I was then in a condition where I could be justified of my sins. I then entered into a covenant relationship with Christ. It was then that I was justified and made perfect in Christ. I was then filled with a wonderful hope of perfection and eternal life. I then began to repent and seek to overcome my sins. Gaining justification occurred within a short period of time as the result of my faith in Christ and a change in the way I thought and felt about sin.

Repentance was much more difficult. Some of the activities I was involved in, such as stealing and gambling, were fairly easy to quit. Upon being born again, I no longer desired to do those things and have never done them since. Some sins were not as easy to stop, however. I had been involved with many acts of immorality for several years. It was a habit. The repeated acts had destroyed my character. It was a long process to change my habits and character. I struggled with some of my sins for years before I finally overcame them. Other sins I still struggle with today and have occasional relapses. However, each time I committed a sin I felt awful. I didn't want to sin, but because of the flesh and the habit and character I had developed; an instant change was not possible, despite my righteous desire for it to be so.

During the process of changing my habits and my character, I was still justified because of my desire to do what was right. The very fact that I grieved over my sins and wanted desperately to overcome them was proof that I and my sins were not living harmoniously together. I had declared war on my sins because I was born again and God's nature was at work in me. Still, sanctification was a slow and gradual process as I worked each day to improve and become more like Christ.

During the process of seeking to change and repent, I remember one instant when I almost gave up trying. I was in continual battle with my sins, and I would continually lose. I had failed so many times I began to wonder if I would ever change. I began to think, "Why should I resist any longer? It would be so much easier just to live in my sins." If I chose to go back to a life of open rebellion, I would have left my covenant relationship with Christ and would have no longer been justified. However, I resisted the temptation to quit and continued to fight and stayed in the covenant. I realized that all I had to do was try my hardest to fight sin and keep God's commands and Christ would save me. Even though my performance was poor, it was still my best. I began to trust in the grace of Christ and His promise to save me rather than trust in my performance. I picked back up the shield of faith and resumed the conflict against sin, confident that I was then clean and acceptable before God because of my covenant relationship with Christ, even though my performance was poor.

Often we think that overcoming our weaknesses is something we must do, but this is just not the case. Christ is the one who will make our weaknesses strengths. All we have to do is continue in the fight against sin, and Christ will make us strong. He doesn't say I will help you make your weaknesses strength. He says He will do it. Our faith is to be in Christ, not in our performance. Our part is to strive to be obedient to God's commands and then have faith that He will keep His promise to make us perfect.

CHAPTER 3

THE PARADOX OF PERFORMANCE

*"But many that are first shall be last; and the
last shall be first."*
—Matthew 19:30, King James Version

Some view life as a class graded on a curve—where your grade depends on how well others in the class perform. A teacher utilizing a curved grading system may give only the top 10 percent of the class As. It doesn't matter how much time they put in or how hard they tried. It only matters that they did better than 90 percent of the class. Only those who are top performers compared to others will receive As. Curves breed a sense of competition and comparison. In the gospel, there is no place for competition and comparison. God's plan is completely individualized; there will be some in the bottom 10 percent in performance compared to others who will receive eternal life. There will be those in the top 10 percent in performance when compared to others who will not receive eternal life, fulfilling the scripture, "But many that are first shall be last; and the last shall be first."[1]

Doing Our Personal Best

"Whatever your hand finds to do, do it with all your might."
—Ecclesiastes 9:10, New International Version

The Lord set the ultimate goal when He said, "Be ye therefore perfect, even as your Father which is in heaven is perfect."[2] As perfection is unattainable while on earth, Christ is more worried about our desire to obtain perfection and our doing our personal best even if this is far from perfection. Sometimes our personal best is not high quality, but if it is our best it is acceptable to the Lord.

The Parable of the Talents

The Lord illustrates this point in the parable of the Talents. In this parable, a lord gave to one of his servants five talents, to another two talents, and to another one talent.[3] The servants who received two and five talents both returned to the lord more talents than he had given them, to which the lord replied, "Well done, [thou] good and faithful servant: thou hast been faithful over a few things, I will make thee ruler over many things: enter thou into the joy of thy lord."[4] The servant who received one talent was afraid and hid his talent in the ground and returned to the lord only the one talent he had received, for which the lord rebuked him saying, "You wicked, lazy servant! . . . You should have put my money on deposit with the bankers, so that when I returned I would have received it back with interest. . . . Throw that worthless servant outside, into the darkness, where there will be weeping and gnashing of teeth."[5] In the parable, there was no comparison between the servants; each received an individual accounting. The servant who received one talent was not punished for having less than the other servants, but he was punished for not doing his personal best. It doesn't matter if your neighbor has greater or fewer talents than you. What matters is what you do with your talents. Life is not a competition with others. Life is a competition with yourself—to each day do your personal best.

The Broken Kneecap

While in college I hyperextended my knee and fractured my

kneecap playing basketball. I was unable to walk and was on crutches. Every Tuesday morning I had a meeting on campus. It usually took me twelve minutes to walk from my apartment to the building where the meeting was, but on the crutches it took me thirty-five minutes. As I made my way to the building, everyone was passing me. I was the slowest person on campus, yet I continued toward the building and eventually made it. Even though it took me almost three times as long, I still made it. I went as fast as I could according to my circumstances and abilities. We cannot judge others in how far they have progressed in the gospel or judge their level of obedience, because we do not know their circumstances and abilities. It would have been foolish for someone to say, "Cameron is a real loser. It took him thirty-five minutes to do something I can do in twelve minutes," or "I am better than Cameron because I can get to the building three times as fast as he can." When you take into consideration my circumstances and abilities (broken kneecap and on crutches), I was doing a good job. The same concept applies to the gospel. We can't judge others, because we don't know their circumstances. We should not ask the question, "How am I doing compared to so and so?" We should ask, "Am I doing my personal best?"

Constantly Seek Improvement

> *"True nobility is in being superior to your own previous self."*
> —Ancient proverb

Satan tries to persuade us to be content with just getting by. The Lord rebukes those who are satisfied with their condition in life, who are content with the way things are, and who don't seek change and improvement. We are always in need of improvement.

If you say "I . . . have need of nothing"[6] and "do not realize that you are wretched, pitiful, poor, blind and naked,"[7] the Lord will see you as being lukewarm (apathetic) and will cast you out, as He said in the book of Revelation, "because you are lukewarm, and neither hot nor cold, I will spit you out of my mouth."[8] The Lord expects us to continually seek improvement.

The Parable of the Fig Tree

The Savior teaches this principle further in the miracle and parable of the Fig Tree found in chapter 11 of Mark. Jesus, walking with His disciples, came to a fig tree that had no figs on it. When Jesus saw that there were no figs upon the fig tree, He cursed the fig tree, and the next day it was withered and dead. This miracle is different from all the other recorded miracles of Jesus that were performed for relief, blessing, and beneficent purposes. This appears to be an act of judgment and destructive execution. A key to understanding this miracle and parable is found in verse 13, which reads, "It was not the season for figs."[9] The fig tree didn't have figs on it because figs were not in season. None of the trees had figs on them, so why did Jesus destroy this tree? On his tape titled "A Higher Standard of Excellence," Mark Gorman states that at 2 a.m. God told him the meaning of these passages. When the inspiration came, he sat straight up in bed and God spoke to him, saying, "If all you are doing is what comes naturally to you, I am not impressed. If you are only producing when everyone else is producing, so what? If you are just keeping up with the crowd, big deal." To impress the Lord, we must strive for excellence and do more than just what comes naturally. We must not just produce fruit when it is in season; we must produce fruit every day. We must rise above mediocrity. We must rise above just getting by. We must excel.

Line upon Line

The Lord gives us a little knowledge, and if we give heed to this knowledge, He will give us more. The prophet Isaiah taught, "But the word of the LORD was unto them precept upon precept, precept upon precept; line upon line, line upon line; here a little, and there a little."[10]

God will allow us to know more than we do presently. This gift enables a person to seek improvement continually without becoming overwhelmed. God reveals a few of our weaknesses so we can have hope in overcoming them. If He revealed all our inadequacies at once we would be devastated. As we overcome some of our faults, we receive more knowledge and we see additional areas that can be improved. As we begin doing what we know to be right, we will learn more. We continue this process of gaining knowledge and aligning our behavior with that knowledge until we have learned to live in accordance with all the principles of success.

A great hindrance to our progression is not living in accordance with the things we know to be right—for those who do not give heed to the knowledge given them will receive no more and will also have taken from them that which they had been given. The Savior teaches this principle, saying, "For whosoever receiveth, to him shall be given, and he shall have more abundance; but whosoever continueth not to receive, from him shall be taken away even that he hath."[11] In the parable of the Fig Tree, Jesus took from the tree which was not producing figs that which it did have (leaves), causing them to wither. The Lord said in the book of Jeremiah that those with "no figs on the tree . . . [will have] what I have given them taken from them."[12]

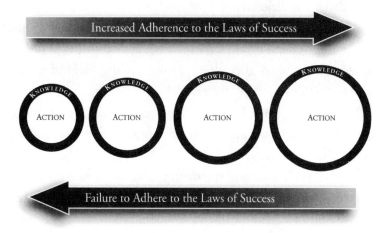

The great football coach Vince Lombardi taught, "Constantly seek ways to do better whatever needs to be done. If a person with this quality will continue positive application of this negative factor, that person will have a leadership role. The quality:

dissatisfaction. To make the unsatisfactory satisfactory or better is the mark of leadership. Never be satisfied with less than top performance, and progress will be the reward." Each time we achieve a goal we should ask, How can it be done better? How can it be improved? "Never [be] satisfied with the status quo or with past attainments. Reaching a goal is merely a signal to set a higher one. Goal-setting is done in small increments so that people never become discouraged: at the same time, they are never permanently satisfied."[13]

Captain James Cook, an eighteenth-century English explorer, showed the spirit of excellence by saying of his many voyages of discovery, "I had an ambition, not only to go farther than any man had ever been before, but I wanted to go as far as it was possible for any man to go."

Christ's Unconditional Love

When I sin, I am at times initially hesitant to go to the Lord and ask for forgiveness. I have a natural tendency to want to hide, as did Adam and Eve after they partook of the forbidden fruit. Genesis 3:8 reads, "And they heard the voice of the Lord God walking in the garden in the cool of the day: and Adam and his wife hid themselves from the presence of the Lord God amongst the trees of the garden."

When I sin, Satan and the natural man work to convince me that if I go to the Lord with my sins, the response from the Lord will be one of disappointment, condemnation, and alienation. Satan will put thoughts into my head such as, "You screwed up again. Do you really think the Lord will forgive you for the 432nd time? You are a failure. You are never going to change, so why try? Just give up." Or with such thoughts as, "Hide so you do not have to experience the disappointment and wrath of the

Lord." You think I would have learned from previous encounters with the Lord seeking forgiveness and examples from the scriptures that this would not be the case. The scriptures are filled with stories of Christ's mercy and forgiveness. The prophet Nehemiah describes Christ as "a God ready to pardon, gracious and merciful, slow to anger, and of great kindness."[14]

Nevertheless I still find that I have to fight the tendency to hide my sins from the Lord. Eventually I get up the courage to go to the Lord in prayer and ask for forgiveness again. Each time I petition the Lord in prayer for forgiveness, I am overwhelmed by His outpouring of love, acceptance, and forgiveness. The Lord declares, "Though your sins be as scarlet, they shall be as white as snow; though they be red like crimson, they shall be as wool. . . . I will forgive . . . and I will remember [your] sin no more."[15]

The book of 1 John states, "If we say that we have no sin, we deceive ourselves, and the truth is not in us. If we confess our sins, [Christ] is faithful and just to forgive us our sins . . . and the blood of Jesus Christ . . . cleanseth us from all sin."[16]

May we each have the strength to resist the temptation to hide from the Lord and have the strength to repent and confess our sins to the Lord, so we may each repeatedly hear the glorious word of the Savior in response to our petition for forgiveness, "Be of good cheer; thy sins be forgiven thee."[17] We never need to hide from the Lord, for His love and acceptance are not based on performance. His love is unconditional.

CHAPTER 4

THE PARADOX OF LEADERSHIP

"He that is greatest among you shall be your servant."
—Matthew 23:11, King James Version

"None of Jesus' leadership lessons may seem more paradoxical than the servant-leader concept. . . . The concept of the servant-leader is difficult for many to grasp today, in part because our leadership literature espouses just the opposite. . . . In the kingdom of God, the way up is down. Jesus overturned contemporary notions of power and replaced them with servant leadership. In a sense He was saying, 'It doesn't matter who has the title. Look for the one with the servant's heart, and there you've found your leader.'"[1]

At times, the apostles struggled to model the principles of leadership the Lord taught and modeled. For example, the Bible recounts the Lord confronting the apostles about an argument they had as follows: "[Jesus] asked them, What was it that ye disputed among yourselves by the way? But they held their peace: for by the way they had disputed among themselves, who should be the greatest. And he sat down, and called the twelve, and saith unto them, If any man desire to be first, the same shall be last of all, and servant of all."[2]

"In the Jewish society of the day—as in most societies in every generation—there was a huge emphasis on power, position, prestige, and titles. 'Who's number one?' is still the operative question. Because He knew their hearts, Jesus knew about their sinful ambition even before he asked what they were arguing about. And like little children caught misbehaving, they were ashamed to answer him. . . . He chose this moment for an unforgettable teaching experience."[3] The Master taught, "He that is greatest among you shall be your servant."[4]

Jesus Christ—The Perfect Leader

Jesus provides us with the perfect model of leadership to follow and learn from. He always focuses on serving others. The New Testament is filled with examples of Christ's service. One such account is the washing of the disciples' feet. "When Jesus laid aside his robe, took up the towel and basin and began washing feet, he did something that was as shocking in his day as it would be in ours. In the time of Jesus, washing other people's feet was . . . the job of a servant. . . . The moment Jesus set the basin in front of the first disciple and began washing the first pair of feet . . . men who had been bragging about their own greatness were stunned into silence."[5]

JESUS WASHES THE FEET OF HIS DISCIPLES.

Another example of Christ's service is found in the account of a man afflicted with leprosy. During biblical times, there was no known cure for the disease, and it was viewed as very contagious. Once an individual contracted leprosy, he was an immediate outcast and excluded from contact with others. The Bible records, "And there came a leper to [Jesus], beseeching him, and kneeling down to him, and saying unto him, If thou wilt, thou canst make me clean. And Jesus, moved with compassion, put forth his hand, and touched him, and saith unto him, I will; be thou clean. And as soon as he had spoken, immediately the leprosy departed from him, and he was cleansed."[6] In this account, the apostle Mark makes note that when Christ spoke, "Be thou clean," the leper was healed. Obviously Christ didn't have to touch this man's disfigured, lesion-filled skin to heal him, and yet Christ chose to touch him anyway, most likely fulfilling the long-unfulfilled need of human touch. Christ not only healed this man, but He served him in a very personal and meaningful way by the way He healed him.

Napoleon Bonaparte said of Christ, "Alexander, Caesar, Charlemagne, and I have founded empires. But on what did we rest the creations of our genius? Upon force. Jesus Christ founded his empire upon love; and at this hour millions would die for him."[7] Many leaders focus on power and control, but Jesus focuses on love and service. Jesus declares, "Ye know that the princes of the Gentiles exercise dominion over them, and they that are great exercise authority upon them. But it shall not be so among you: but whosoever will be great among you, let him be your minister; And whosoever will be chief among you, let him be your servant: Even as the Son of man came not to be ministered unto, but to minister."[8]

Father Damien de Veuster

In 1865 an epidemic of leprosy broke out in Hawaii. The Hawaiian government passed the Act to Prevent the Spread of Leprosy, which quarantined lepers to the island of Moloka'i. At the time there was no cure for the disease, so the leprosy victims were separated from their family and friends and banished to Moloka'i.

"The ships with their human cargo would anchor offshore, and the lepers were forced overboard to either swim to the rocky shore or drown. Those who survived lived in caves or in shacks made of leaves and branches. The lepers huddled together, condemned and without hope. An occasional supply ship would toss crates of food into the water, which the currents would wash ashore for the lepers to retrieve, but the government provided no shelter or drinking water. Seven years after the leper colony on Moloka'i was founded, a Belgian priest, Father Damien de Veuster, volunteered to serve there. He arrived in 1873 only thirty-three years old, and he lived among the lepers. Skilled in carpentry and medicine, he helped the lepers to build decent houses, treated their degenerating bodies and buried their dead."[9] Father Damien was a compassionate servant of Christ who laid down his life for the outcasts of his day. His life is an example of what it truly means to be a servant-leader.

Revolutionary Patriots

The signing of the Declaration of Independence by the American colonies was a solemn act that required great firmness, patriotism, and sacrifice. It was treason against the government of Great Britain—an offense that was punishable by death. At the signing, Benjamin Franklin is quoted as having replied to a comment by John Hancock that they must all hang together, saying, "Yes, we must, indeed, all hang together, or most assuredly we shall all hang separately."[10] This play on words suggested that if they failed to stay united and win the revolution, they would surely each be tried and executed, individually, for treason. By unanimous vote the Declaration was adopted, with each signer pledging his life, fortunes, and sacred honor to the fight for freedom.

The Declaration of Independence was official, but the fight for freedom was just beginning. The Revolutionary War continued on for seven more years. On August 8, 1776, General George Washington wrote the soldiers saying, "Allow me, therefore, to address you as fellow citizens and fellow soldiers engaged in the same glorious cause. . . . There can be no doubt, that success will crown our efforts, if we firmly and resolutely determine to conquer or to die. . . . We must now determine to be enslaved or free. If we make freedom our choice, we must obtain it by the blessing of Heaven on our united and vigorous efforts. I salute you, Gentlemen, most affectionately, and beg leave to remind you, that liberty, honor and safety are all at stake; and I trust Providence will smile upon our efforts, and establish us once more, the inhabitants of a free and happy country. I am, Gentlemen, your humble servant."[11]

Two hundred and seventeen thousand American service members fought during the eight-year Revolutionary War.[12] They suffered much sickness, privations, hardships, and death, but their courage, desire for freedom, and reliance on the Almighty led them to an eventual victory. Just over 6,800 of these men died in battle, and "about 25,000 became prisoners of war, most of them confined in New York City under conditions so atrocious that they perished by the thousands. Evidence suggests that at least 17,500 Americans [70 percent of those imprisoned] died in these prisons."[13]

The American officers captured by the British were crowded so tightly into prisons that at night as they slept on the hard floor they could only change position by turning all at once. The minimal food provided was of the poorest kind. Those kept in the prison ships were forced by the thousands into the hulls of the ship where it was near impossible to sleep with the putrid air, stifling heat, and groans of the dying. Each morning the harsh order came below, "Rebels, turn out your dead." The dead were selected from the living and conveyed in a boat to the shore by their companions, under guard, and hastily buried.[14]

The prisoners were viewed as traitors who had committed treason against the Crown, which was punishable by hanging. "The most outrageous of all the crimes committed . . . was the hanging of 275 American prisoners of war without trial and in utter repudiation of all existing articles of war. . . . All of these Patriots could have betrayed the cause of liberty and independence in exchange for their lives, but preferred death. All they had to do was to sign a document of allegiance to the Crown and receive a free pardon by enlisting in His Majesty's Army or Navy."[15] Not one of these prisoners betrayed the cause of liberty and independence to save his life.

"The imprisoned and dying patriots, in the dark hours of 1780, when nearly all hope of independence had fled forever, and when the deserter and traitor stalked over the land in fearful combination, reached forth their skeleton hands, wrote, and bequeathed this task to their countrymen in their dying hours: 'If you are victorious, and our country emerges free and independent from the contest in which she is now engaged, but the end of which we are not permitted to see, bury us in her soil, and engrave our names on the monument you shall erect over our bones, as victims who willingly surrendered their lives as a portion of the price paid for your liberties, and our departed spirits will never murmur, or regret the sacrifice we made to obtain for you the blessings you enjoy.'"[16]

The last major battle of the Revolutionary War was the battle of Yorktown, when American and French forces achieved a large and decisive victory over the British, capturing over seven thousand of the British troops and forcing an unconditional surrender by General Lord Cornwallis on October 17, 1781. During the surrender, the British drummers played the march, "The Day the World Turned Upside Down." The surrender of Cornwallis's army prompted the British government to eventually negotiate an end to the conflict. In 1783 the Treaty of Paris officially ended the Revolutionary War.

Following victory in the Revolutionary War, the American colonies had the unique opportunity of establishing a new country and government. The Articles of Confederation were the first governing document that loosely tied the newly independent thirteen colonies, but they were incomplete and inadequate to completely govern the new nation. To establish a constitution and a new form of government, the Constitutional Convention was organized and held in Philadelphia from May 25 to September 17, 1787. George Washington presided over the convention, and with fifty-four other great leaders of the new nation and the inspiration of the Almighty, they drafted the Constitution of the United States of America. This document was the first written constitution in the world and the foundation of the newly founded republic.

James Madison, often called the father of the Constitution for the key role he played at the convention, said of the fifty-five leaders assembled, "I feel it a duty to express my profound and solemn conviction, derived from my intimate opportunity of observing and appreciating the views of the Convention, collectively and individually, that there never was an assembly of men, charged with a great and arduous trust, who were more pure in their motives, or more exclusively or anxiously devoted to the object committed to them, than were the members of the [Constitutional] Convention of 1787, to the devising and proposing a constitutional system . . . [to] secure the permanent liberty and happiness of their country."[17]

There were desires by some to make Washington king. The first Congress voted to pay Washington a salary of twenty-five thousand dollars a year (approximately five hundred thousand dollars in 2010 dollars). Washington, however, chose to continue his work as an unpaid servant of the people. During his years as commander-in-chief of the Continental Army he took no pay. He would do the same during his eight years as the first president of the United States. He exemplified the word of the Savior,

"But he that is greatest among you shall be your servant."[18] Abigail Adams, wife of John Adams, wrote of Washington, "No man ever lived, more deservedly beloved and respected. . . . [He] maintained a modest diffidence of his own talents. . . . Possesst of power, possesst of an extensive influence, he never used it but for the benefit of his Country."

An order from General Washington during the war reads, "The fate of unborn millions will now depend, under God, on the courage and conduct of this army. . . . Let us therefore rely upon the goodness of the cause, and the aid of the Supreme Being, in whose hands victory is."[19] The Founding Fathers and revolutionary soldiers fought and worked diligently not for power, position, fame, or fortune but as servants of "the people" to secure for millions yet unborn a free country filled with life, liberty, and the pursuit of happiness.

Abraham Lincoln

Abraham Lincoln, like his predecessor George Washington, was a servant to the people. Lincoln exemplified the heart of a servant throughout his life. During his youth, when one evening, he was "returning from a 'raising' in his wide neighborhood, with a number of companions, he discovered a straying horse, with saddle and bridle upon him. The horse was recognized as belonging to a man who was accustomed to excess in drink, and it was suspected at once that the owner was not far off. A short search only was necessary to confirm the suspicions of the young men. The poor drunkard was found in a perfectly helpless condition, upon the chilly ground. Abraham's companions urged the cowardly policy of leaving him to his fate, but young Lincoln would not hear to the proposition. At [Lincoln's] request, the miserable [drunkard] was lifted on his shoulders, and he actually carried him [1/4 of a mile] to the nearest house. Sending word to his father that he should not be back that night, with the reason for his absence, he attended and nursed the man until the morning."[20]

When Lincoln saw others in need, he did everything he could to assist them, even at his own expense and sacrifice. He exemplified this attitude in his profession, and as a servant to the people when in public office. A simple story shows his heart. "He was riding . . . [when] he saw a pig struggling, and with such faint efforts that it was evident that he could not extricate himself from the mud. Mr. Lincoln looked at the pig and the mud which enveloped him, and then looked at some new clothes with which he had but a short time before enveloped himself. Deciding against the claims of the pig, he rode on, but he could not get rid of the vision of the poor brute, and, at last, after riding two miles, he turned back, determined to rescue the animal at the expense of his new clothes. Arrived at the spot, he tied his horse, and cooly went to work to build of old rails a passage to the bottom of the hole. Descending on these rails, he seized the pig and dragged him out, but not without serious damage to the clothes he wore."[21]

Lincoln's Rise to Leadership

"At England's University of Kent, economists and psychologists undertook what they call a cooperation game, where you gather a bunch of people and give each person cash. The subjects decide how much of the cash they'll put into a common fund in the middle of the room. Now the best thing for everybody to do is to put in all their money, because the researchers tell them that all the money collected in the common fund will be doubled and divided equally among all participants. But the dominant strategy for people who are selfish is to hold everything back and let the 'suckers' put in their money, because then they'll keep all the money given to them and get a good share of the others' too. In the second phase of this experiment the researchers had the subjects solve puzzles in teams, and they each had to elect a team leader. In 88 percent of the cases, the team leader who was selected was the biggest giver to the common fund. The researchers realized that . . . giving is a leadership trait people observe in one another."[22]

Lincoln did not aspire to leadership positions but was elected by his peers because of his servant nature. "In the threatening aspect of affairs at the time of the Black Hawk War, Governor Reynolds issued a call for volunteers . . . and Lincoln . . . was first to enlist. The company being full, they held a meeting at Richland for the election of officers. Lincoln had won many hearts and they told him that he must be their captain. It was an office that he did not aspire to, and one for which he felt that he had no special fitness; but he consented to be a candidate. There was but one other candidate for the office (a Mr. Kirkpatrick), and he was one of the most influential men in the county. Previously, Kirkpatrick had been an employer of Lincoln, and was so overbearing in his treatment of the young man that the latter left him. The simple mode of electing their captain, adopted by the company, was by placing the candidates apart, and telling the men to go and stand with the one they preferred. Lincoln and his competitor took their positions, and then the word was given. At least three out of every four went to Lincoln at once. When it was seen by those who had ranged themselves with the other candidate that Lincoln was the choice of the majority of the company, they left their places, one by one, and came over to the successful side, until Lincoln's opponent in the friendly strife was left standing almost alone."[23]

He maintained his role as servant throughout the various positions to which he would be elected. As president of the United States, Lincoln often concluded his letter with the phrases, "Your friend and servant," "Your obedient servant," and "Your humble servant,"[24] and in the White House, he never alluded to himself as "president" and he asked others to call him "Lincoln" instead of "Mr. President."[25]

During the Civil War, a clergyman said to Lincoln, "I hope the Lord is on our side." Lincoln replied, "I am not at all concerned about that for I know that the Lord is always on the side of the right. But it is my constant anxiety and prayer that this nation should be on the Lord's side."[26] Lincoln worked diligently to do that which was right without concern for power, position, and popularity. When signing the Emancipation Proclamation, which led to the eventual freedom of millions of slaves, Lincoln said, "I never, in my life, felt more certain that I was doing right, than I do in signing this paper."[27]

"On the Monday before the assassination, when the President was on his way from Richmond, he stopped at City Point. Calling upon the head surgeon at that place, Mr. Lincoln told him that he wished to visit all the hospitals under his charge and shake hands with every soldier. The surgeon asked if he knew what he was undertaking, there being five or six thousand soldiers at that place, and it would be quite a tax upon his strength to visit all the wards and shake hands with every soldier. Mr. Lincoln answered with a smile [that] . . . he wanted them to know that he appreciated what they had done for their country. . . . The surgeon began his rounds with the President, who walked from bed to bed, extending his hand to all, saying a few words of sympathy to some, making kind inquiries of others, and welcomed by all with the heartiest cordiality. As they passed along they came to a ward in which lay a rebel who had been wounded and was a prisoner. As the tall figure of the kindly visitor appeared in sight, he was recognized by the rebel soldier, who, raising himself on his elbow in bed, watched Mr. Lincoln as he approached and extending his hand exclaimed, while tears ran down his cheeks: 'Mr. Lincoln, I have long wanted to see you, to ask your forgiveness for ever raising my hand against the old flag.' Mr. Lincoln was moved to tears. He heartily shook the hand of the repentant rebel and assured him of his good will, and with a few words of kind advice."[28] After many hours, Lincoln had visited each and every solider.

Lincoln is today honored as one of the United States' greatest presidents, even though he had no concern for such praise. Lincoln just wanted to serve his country and do what was right. Following is one of the many tributes written regarding Abraham Lincoln after his death:

To the memory of Abraham Lincoln, President
of the United States of America, who died a
martyr to his country, falling under the hand of
a traitor assassin on the night of the 14th day of
April 1865. The fourth anniversary of the
beginning of the great War of Rebellion,
through which he led the nation to a glorious
triumph. Just completed when the dastardly
revenge of vanquished treason was wrought in
this monstrous murder. The Great Republic
loved him as its Father, and reverenced him as
the preserver of its national life. The oppressed
people of all lands looked up to him as the
anointed of liberty, and hailed in him the con-
secrated leader of her cause. He struck the
chains of slavery from four millions . . . with a
noble faith in humanity. . . By his wisdom, his
prudence, his calm temper, his steadfast
patience, his lofty courage, and his loftier faith,
he saved the Republic from dissolution. By his
simple integrity, he illustrated the neglected
principles of its Constitution, and restored
them to their just ascendancy. By all the results
of his administration of its government, he
inaugurated a New Era in the history of
mankind. The wisdom of his statesmanship was
excelled only by its virtuousness. Exercising a
power which surpassed that of kings, he bore
himself always as the servant of the people, and
never its master.[29]

Conclusion

"I once met a woman who owns a phenomenally successful executive recruiting company. When I asked her what her secret was, she said, 'It's simple. Whenever the phone rings, I say to myself. 'That's God on the line,' and then I think about all the ways I can serve that person.'"[30] Jesus Christ provides us with the perfect model of leadership. To lead as the master Jesus Christ leads, we must be humble servants.

CHAPTER 5

THE PARADOX OF WISDOM

"Professing themselves to be wise, they became fools. . . ."
"Let him become a fool, that he may be wise."
—Romans 1:22; 1 Corinthians 3:18, King James Version

If we seek to use our own ideas and the ideas of the world to guide our lives, we will become fools. Once we realize that we are fools without God and recognize that God is the source of truth, we can gain wisdom. Truth is not invented or created, but discovered. Galileo observed, "All truths are easy to understand once they are discovered; the point is to discover them." So how is truth discovered? By going to the Lord in humility and asking Him to impart to us His wisdom. As we seek Christ to guide us, we will be wise. The Bible declares, "Trust in the Lord with all thine heart; and lean not unto thine own understanding. In all thy ways acknowledge him, and he shall direct thy paths."[1]

Three Lessons Learned from a Talking Donkey

In the Old Testament we find the story of Balaam, his donkey, and the angel of the Lord. "Balaam was riding his donkey to Moab, and two of his servants were with him. But God was angry that Balaam had gone, so one of the LORD's angels stood in the road to stop him. When Balaam's donkey saw the angel standing there with a sword, it walked off the road and into an open field. Balaam had to beat the donkey to get it back on the road. Then the angel stood between two vineyards, in a narrow path with a stone wall on each side. When the donkey saw the angel, it walked so close to one of the walls that Balaam's foot scraped against the wall. Balaam beat the donkey again. The angel moved once more and stood in a spot so narrow that there was no room for the donkey to go around. So it just lay down. Balaam lost his temper, then picked up a stick and smacked the donkey. When that happened, the LORD told the donkey to speak, and it asked Balaam, "What have I done to you that made you beat me three times?"

"You made me look stupid!" Balaam answered. "If I had a sword, I'd kill you here and now!"

"But you're my owner," replied the donkey, "and you've ridden me many times. Have I ever done anything like this before?"

"No," Balaam admitted.

Just then, the LORD let Balaam see the angel standing in the road, holding a sword, and Balaam bowed down.

The angel said, "You had no right to treat your donkey like that! I was the one who blocked your way, because I don't think you should go to Moab. If your donkey had not seen me and stopped those three times, I would have killed you and let the donkey live."

Balaam replied, "I was wrong. I didn't know you were trying to stop me. If you don't think I should go, I'll return home right now."[2]

There are three extremely valuable lessons we can learn from this story.

Lesson 1: You Must Learn to Effectively Receive Criticism and Correction

"Stern discipline awaits him who leaves the path; he who hates correction will die."
—Proverbs 15:10, New International Version

When others correct us, there is a natural tendency to get upset and metaphorically hit a donkey. In response the person correcting us will say, as did Balaam's donkey, "Why are you getting mad at me? I am just trying to help you." The Bible states, "You can trust a friend who corrects you, but kisses from an enemy are nothing but lies."[3] A true friend will tell us when we are off course or need correction even though it is not what we want to hear. Their love and concern for our well-being will supersede the natural desire to avoid the conflict or ignore the issue. As states the Sicilian proverb, "Only your real friends will tell you when your face is dirty."

The Lord will correct us when we get off course. The apostle Paul wrote, "God disciplines us for our good."[4] "For the Lord disciplines the one he loves."[5] Discipline and correction help us get back on track when we have strayed. "Despise not the chastening of the Lord; neither be weary of his correction."[6] The quicker we can recognize we are wrong, the more quickly we can get on the right path. A Wal-Mart executive said of Sam Walton, "He is less afraid of being wrong than anyone I've ever known. And once he sees he's wrong, he just shakes it off and heads in another direction."

Lesson 2: You Can Learn Something from Every Person You Meet—Even a Jackass

When someone tries to teach us something we think we already know, there is a natural tendency to get upset and metaphorically hit a donkey. The weakest part of each person is often where he thinks himself the wisest. In the words of the great basketball coach John Wooden, "It's what we learn after we think we know it all that really counts."

There is something we can learn from each person we meet. "If we operate with the assumption that we do not have all the answers or insights, we allow ourselves to value the different viewpoints, judgments, and experiences others may bring."[7] Each person has unique insights and experiences we can draw upon. We should approach others with an open mind and a willingness to be taught. We should try to look for the good in others, and we should try to learn from all others as much as possible.

The Bloody Sash

During the French and Indian War, the British general Edward Braddock, age sixty at the time, employed the help of a Virginia militia. When one of the young Virginian soldiers who was well acquainted with the Indian mode of warfare modestly offered his advice, the haughty Braddock said, "What! An American buskin teach a British general how to fight!"[8] Braddock did not heed the advice, and the British suffered a disastrous defeat. General Braddock was wounded by a shot through the right arm and into his lung. Following the injury to General Braddock, that same twenty-three-year-old Virginia soldier, with no official position in the chain of command, was able to lead and maintain some order and formed a rear guard, which allowed them to evacuate and eventually disengage. This action earned him the title of "Hero of the Monongahela." General Braddock was carried off the field by George Washington, the soldier whose advice he had rejected. Braddock died on July 13, 1755, four days after the battle. Before he died, Braddock left Washington the blood-stained sash of his uniform. Washington carried the sash with him for the remainder of his life. Perhaps he carried the sash as a reminder of the cost of pride and of the necessity of being humble and teachable if he was to be successful in his efforts. Had Braddock listened to the advice of young George Washington, his life may have been saved.

George Washington was teachable and spent time each day learning from others. During his lifetime, Washington accumulated a library of more than seven hundred books, a great many of which he studied closely. Washington's step-granddaughter, Nelly Custis, wrote to one of Washington's early biographers, "It was his custom to retire to his library at nine or ten o'clock, where he remained an hour before he went to his chamber. He always arose before the sun, and remained in his library until called to breakfast."

Lesson 3: If the Path You Are on Is Blocked, the Lord May Want You to Go in a Different Direction

When the path we are trying to take is blocked, there is a natural tendency to get upset and metaphorically hit a donkey. My first business venture failed, leaving me with thousands of dollars in business debt. I was newly married, and I had no income. My wife was working earning ten dollars per hour, but her income was not even enough to cover our eighteen hundred dollars a month in debt payments. I now joke with her that she married me for my money, but the truth is I had less than nothing because of the burden of debt. I was forced to put my entrepreneurial efforts on hold for a season and look for a job. I graduated with honors from business school and applied for dozens of jobs that were a good match for my skills, experience, and degree, but I received rejection letter after rejection letter. I even applied at a call center that seemed to hire nearly everyone for a six-dollar-per-hour job and was rejected. I now joke with people, "I had to start a business because I was the only person who would hire me."

I prayed to the Lord for help finding a job but got the answer that the Lord did not want me to get a job. I was supposed to start a business. This did not seem to make any sense at this point in my life and did not seem like an option. I followed a prompting to start a lecture series at a university, which my wife supported even though it didn't seem to make any sense since it would take a significant amount of my time and would provide no income. Acting in faith, we built the lecture series, in which I and guests I invited in taught. Following one of the lectures by an invited guest, a miracle happened. It was about one and a half hours after the lecture had ended since I had stayed to talk with students and answer questions. When I exited the building, the guest lecturer pulled up next to me in the parking lot. He rolled down his window and said, "The Spirit told me I needed to come back to talk to you." We set up a time to meet. We began the meeting with prayer but were not sure exactly why we were meeting. He laid out the projects he was working on and ideas he wanted to pursue. I laid out my talents and experience and the projects I was working on and wanted to pursue. We eventually came to a business idea that felt like the right one. I prayed about this venture and received a clear answer from the Lord that this is what I was supposed to do. We partnered on the new venture, with him putting up all the money and me putting up the time to build and manage the company. The company did over $1 million in revenue the second year in business and over $10 million in the fifth year of business. What had seemed impossible became a reality through Christ. The Lord had blocked the job path because there was another path I was to take.

Conclusion

Long before Shrek had his run-in with a talking donkey, Balaam had his life saved by one. If you apply the three lessons discussed above, you, too, will have a story to share about the time your life was saved by a talking donkey. "Listen to advice and accept instruction, and in the end you will be wise."[9]

CHAPTER 6

THE PARADOX OF RECEIVING

*"For whosoever receiveth, to him shall be given,
and he shall have more abundance; but whosoever
continueth not to receive, from him shall be taken
away even that he hath."*
—Matthew 13:10–11, Inspired Version

The Lord illustrates the paradox of receiving in the parable of the Talents. In this parable, a lord gave to one of his servants five talents, to another two talents, and to another one talent.[1]

The servant who received two talents and the servant who received five talents both received more talents; however, the servant who received one talent hid the talent and received no more. When the day of reckoning arrived the servant given two talents and the servant given five talents both reported increasing the number of talents they had received, to which the lord said, "Well done, thou good and faithful servant: thou hast been faithful over a few things, I will make thee ruler over many things: enter thou into the joy of thy lord."[2] The servant who had hidden his talent and as a result received no more received the rebuke, "Thou wicked and slothful servant."[3] The lord then took the talent from him and gave it to the man who had increased his five talents to ten talents and declared, "For unto every one that hath shall be given, and he shall have abundance: but from him that hath not shall be taken away even that which he hath."[4]

Stairs Analogy

Coach John Wooden said, "If I am ever through learning, I am through. You either have to go forward or you'll go backward. You rarely move rapidly upward, but you can go downward very fast." Life cannot be likened to traveling on a stairway, where you can reach a certain step and then stop and maintain your position. Rather, life is more appropriately compared to traveling upward on a downward escalator. If you're not stepping up (putting forth effort), you're really going down. Just as a tree is either growing or decaying, so we are either progressing or digressing. In life, you cannot be at a standstill.

Cup Analogy

The Lord has so many blessings that He wants to pour upon us, but we have to be willing and able to receive them. For example, let's say God has one gallon of gifts He wants to pour upon you, and the cup you have to receive these gifts is big enough to hold one-tenth of a gallon. Your cup will be filled to capacity, but will not be able to hold the other nine-tenths of a gallon of gifts the Lord has for you. As you increase the capacity of your cup, the Lord will continue to fill it. Your cup will always be full to the amount you are able and willing to receive. Some with a one-tenth-of-a-gallon cup may mistakenly think, "My cup is full. I don't need to receive anymore." However, if this ever becomes your attitude, your cup will shrink, and the capacity will decrease and some of the gifts and blessing you previously had will slip over the top of the cup and be lost. We need to continually work to increase the size of our cup so we can receive more and more of the blessings and gifts the Lord wants to pour upon us.

Becoming a Good Receiver

God wants to give us so many wonderful gifts and blessings. Christ declares, "I am come that they might have life, and that they might have it more abundantly."[5] We must learn to be good receivers and accept God's gifts. A rejected gift hurts both the giver and the receiver because the receiver gives up the joy of the gift, and the giver is denied the joy and blessings of giving the gift.

Don't Rob Me of My Blessings

While serving in a missionary ministry in Hawaii, I associated with many wonderful Christians. The Polynesians regarded representatives of Christ with the same respect and honor as they did their chiefs. As I preached the gospel, people of all denominations would impart to us of their time, food, possessions, and money in support of the Lord's work. They knew the Lord would bless them for their sacrifices.

On one particular occasion, when I was walking along the Kamehameha Highway, a car pulled up right alongside me. As we were both in motion, a man rolled down his window and handed me a twenty-dollar bill. At first I didn't realize what he was handing me, but when I found that it was money, I kindly refused and tried to return it. As I ran after the car the man said, "Don't rob me of my blessings." He sped away leaving me with a twenty-dollar bill I felt I shouldn't have. Receiving gifts and money became a regular occurrence. Being new to Hawaii and not fully understanding the culture, I tried to refuse gifts and money that were constantly offered me. I quickly learned not to do this. Each time I tried to refuse the gifts, the giver would get upset and say, "Don't rob me of my blessings!" I learned that by humbly accepting gifts, I could, in turn, faithfully declare that the giver would be blessed for his or her sacrifice.

The Polynesians believed that the more a representative of Christ ate, the more blessings they would receive. Joe, a three-hundred-pound Tongan, took me out to eat, and I ate until I couldn't eat another bite. After we finished, Joe went to the cashier to pay for the meals. As Joe began to pay, the cashier said, "Sir, someone has already paid for the meals." Joe looked around the restaurant and called out loudly, "Who robbed me of my blessings?" The restaurant went quiet. Joe was disappointed that he had not been able to pay for the meals because he believed in the scripture in Acts 20:35 that says, "It is more blessed to give than to receive." In an attempt to still receive blessings for feeding a representative of Christ, he told the cashier that we were going to eat again and this time not to let anyone else pay for the meals. This experience taught me to be a good receiver, although I had trouble at times expanding my stomach far enough to receive all the gifts.

Rejecting Compliments

During the summer I enjoy boating and waterskiing. A few friends and I were headed out to the lake one day, and as we were in front of my house getting the boat ready, one of them said, "I love your yard. It is beautiful." I replied, "Not really. There are so many weeds and so much trimming that needs to be done." He then said again, "No, really, I like your yard." At this point I realized I had rejected his compliment, and he was trying to give the compliment again to see if I would accept it on the second attempt. I accepted the compliment with a simple "Thank you." As I analyzed why I rejected the first compliment, I realized that it was because I didn't think the yard was worthy or deserving of the compliment. In an attempt to reject the compliment, I came up with reasons that the yard was unworthy and undeserving of the compliment.

An important exchange occurs when compliments are given and received. When you reject a compliment, the giver of the compliment might also feel that you are rejecting him or her. This can create awkward exchanges. Imagine, for example, what would occur if someone handed you a beautifully wrapped present and you handed it back and said, "I don't want it."

Some people have learned to be polite by saying "Thank you" to the giver, but in their mind they still reject the compliment with reasons that they are unworthy or undeserving of it. These people have learned how to not insult the giver but are still poor receivers.

Ask and Ye Shall Receive

In one of my first business ventures, I experienced a major setback and was forced to move out of my apartment. My brother had an empty room in his house and agreed to let me stay with him. I knew I could make do with the few possessions I had, but I lacked a bed and dresser. I knelt in prayer and asked the Lord to please provide me with a bed and a small dresser. The next morning, when I went outside, I found in front of the house a bed and a small dresser. I looked at the items with amazement and thankfulness. I moved the items into my room and knelt to thank the Lord for answering my prayer and providing me with these wonderful gifts. Had I not asked the Lord in prayer for the dresser and bed, slept on the floor, and kept my clothes in a box, the story may have gone something like this:

Parable of the Heavenly Warehouse™

Years later I died and went to heaven. When I arrived at the pearly gates, I asked Peter for a tour of heaven. While on the tour, I saw a large warehouse in the distance. I pointed toward it and asked, "Peter, what is that warehouse for?"

Peter replied, "We will not be visiting the warehouse on the tour."

"Why not?" I asked.

Peter replied, "Because the warehouse has to do with your life on earth and will only result in disappointment. We never take new arrivals to their warehouses."

I curiously asked, "What is inside the warehouse?"

Peter answered, "Trust me. You do not want to know. You will be much happier in heaven if you don't know what's inside."

Peter insisted that I forget about the warehouse and continued the tour. I could not stop thinking about the warehouse, and eventually curiosity got the best of me. I ran toward it, opened the door, and entered. What I saw amazed me. Hundreds of shelves lined the warehouse from wall to wall and floor to ceiling. Each shelf was covered with beautifully wrapped gifts of all shapes and sizes. I approached one shelf and found that each of the gifts had my name on it. By this time, Peter had also entered the warehouse.

I turned to him and asked, "What are all these gifts with my name on them?"

Peter took me by the arm and led me to a shelf that contained two large presents and asked me to open them. I unwrapped the presents to find a bed and a dresser.

Somewhat puzzled I asked, "What are these for?"

Peter replied, "Do you remember when you moved in with your brother and needed a bed and a dresser? This is the bed and dresser God wanted to give you."

I then hesitantly asked, "What are all the other presents?"

Peter answered, "These are all the blessings and gifts God wanted to give to you while you were on earth that you did not receive."

I asked Peter, "God knew I needed and wanted a bed and a dresser? So why didn't He give them to me?"

Peter replied, "Let me teach you how the warehouse works." He then took me to an area in which all the shelves were empty.

I asked, "What was on these shelves?"

"On these shelves we kept all the blessings and gifts God gave to you which required no effort or work on your part. Thus, the shelves are all empty, because you received them all while you were on earth," answered Peter.

I anxiously asked, "Well, what about all the other shelves full of gifts? Why wasn't I given them?"

Peter answered, "Some of the gifts required work or effort on your part before you could obtain them."

We walked to a section of the warehouse, and Peter had me look closer at the tags on the gifts. As I looked at the tags I saw my name, and under my name was written the requirement in order for me to receive the gift. The first tag read, "Pray and ask for it." I looked at each tag only to find that they all read, "Pray and ask for it."

I said to Peter, "You mean all I had to do to receive all these gifts in the warehouse was to pray and ask for them?"

Peter replied, "You are getting ahead of me. This section of the warehouse contains all the gifts God wanted to give you and all that was required to receive them was to pray and ask for them. Heaven has warehouses full of undelivered gifts because many have not learned that God has countless gifts to give if one will only ask. My fellow apostle James taught, 'Ye have not, because ye ask not.'[6]"

"Peter, how was I supposed to ask for these gifts when I didn't even know they existed?" I asked.

Peter said, "Here is the next principle of effective prayer. You must pray and ask to know what to pray for."

"What do you mean?" I asked.

Peter answered, "You need to pray to find out what is in your warehouse. You should pray and ask God to tell you what gifts to pray and ask for. It is a wise man who knows what to pray for, and you can know what to pray for by the Spirit, 'for we know not what we should pray for as we ought: but the Spirit itself maketh intercession for us with groanings which cannot be uttered.'[7]"

"This is all very interesting, but there is something I still do not understand. My warehouse is full of gifts, yet there were times on earth when I prayed and asked for things but did not receive them. Can you please explain this?" I inquired.

Peter answered, "It could have been one of two reasons. Either you were asking for something that was not in your warehouse,[8] or what you were asking for required more than simply asking to receive."

To demonstrate his point, Peter took me to another section of the warehouse and said, "As I mentioned earlier, God has placed a requirement for the receipt of each of these gifts. When you receive any gift from God, it is a result of fulfilling this requirement. Asking in prayer is only one of many possible requirements."

I began to look at the tags on the gifts in this section and found the requirements: get married, attend church, start a business, care for the poor, and visit a widow. Some of the gifts contained a long series of requirements to obtain the gift.

As I looked at the many tags, Peter began to relate an experience from his earthly ministry: "One day a man brought his son who was possessed of a devil to me and the other disciples and asked us to cure him, but we were unable to. Then Jesus came and rebuked the devil, and the child was cured that very hour. Later the other disciples and I asked Jesus, 'Why were we unable to cast out the devil and cure the child?' To which Jesus replied, 'Howbeit this kind goeth not out but by prayer and fasting.'[9] From this experience, I learned that gifts can require more than asking to receive them.

"Before I leave you to return to the pearly gates, I have one last principle to teach you," Peter said. "Once you understand that God is your Father and you are His child, many of the difficulties of prayer and receiving gifts will disappear. Once you view God as your Father who wants to bless you, prayer and accepting His gifts become natural and instinctive. As taught the Savior, 'Or what man is there of you, whom if his son ask bread, will he give him a stone? Or if he ask a fish, will he give him a serpent? If ye then, being evil, know how to give good gifts unto your children, how much more shall your Father which is in heaven give good things to them that ask him?'[10] Prayer takes effort, and is an appointed means for obtaining the greatest of God's gifts. Prayer is not to tell God which blessings and gifts he should give you, but to ask for gifts that God is already willing to give and is simply waiting for you to ask for. 'Ask, and it shall be given you; seek, and ye shall find; knock, and it shall be opened unto you.'[11]"

CHAPTER 7

THE PARADOX OF PAIN

"Consider it pure joy . . . whenever you face
trials of many kinds."
—James 1:2, New International Version

The fact that we should rejoice over pain is definitely a gospel paradox. When we experience pain, our natural tendency is not to rejoice but to avoid and despise pain. Since the fall of Adam and Eve in the garden, the earth has been filled with thorns and weeds. The Lord spoke to Adam saying, "By the sweat of your brow you will eat your food."[1]

Is the fact that the earth is filled with weeds and requires pain and hard work to sustain our lives a bad thing? Would life be better if there were no adversity, pain, or opposition? The Lord created a world of opposition for our benefit. He told Adam, "Cursed is the ground for thy sake."[2] Life was not designed to be an existence of endless bliss. Life was designed to create greatness in each of us. Pain, trials, and afflictions are for our good. The Bible declares, "A great trial of affliction . . . [will] abound unto . . . riches";[3] "The trial of your faith [is] much more precious than . . . gold";[4] and "Think it not strange concerning the fiery trial . . . but rejoice . . . [and] be glad also with exceeding joy."[5] The prophet Isaiah teaches that adversity and affliction are good for the growth of our spirit, like bread and water are good for the growth of the body: "The Lord give[s] you the bread of adversity, and the water of affliction."[6] The

Lord declares, "In the world ye shall have tribulation: but be of good cheer."[7]

Myth: Bad Things Should Not Happen to Good People

The myth that bad things should not happen to good people is found among congregations today and by Christians in the Old and New Testaments. A friend of our family told me about a faithful Christian in a neighboring state whose home was burned down. When this individual went to church the following Sunday, a member of her congregation asked her what she had done wrong to deserve such a thing.

In the Old Testament the story is told of a righteous man named Job who "was perfect and upright, and one that feared God, and eschewed evil."[8] Despite his righteousness, Job's children were killed, his property destroyed, and his body afflicted with boils. Job's friend Eliphaz tries to explain Job's great suffering as the result of Job's wickedness and sins.[9]

The Savior corrected the disciples who believed a man was blind as a result of sin. The account in the New Testament reads, "As Jesus passed by, he saw a man which was blind from his birth. And his disciples asked him, saying, Master, who did sin, this man, or his parents, that he was born blind? Jesus answered, Neither hath this man sinned, nor his parents."[10]

Just as the disciples believed the man's blindness could have only been caused by sin, we often assume that sin is the only cause of bad things in our lives. There are multiple reasons that things we usually define as bad (such as pain, suffering, trials, afflictions, and hardships) occur in our lives. To help us understand why bad things happen to good people, I have identified four causes of pain. Personal sin is only one of the four causes of pain. Often one of the other three causes of pain is the reason bad things happen to good people.

Four Causes of Pain ™

1. Liberty
2. Growth
3. Personal Choices/Sins
4. Choices/Sins of Others

When we experience pain, sometimes it is important to ask why it happened. Identifying which of the four causes led to the pain can determine how we respond to it, how we interpret it, and how we feel about it.

Liberty: Cause of Pain No. 1

Four principles must be in force for there to be liberty:

1. Laws ordained by God
2. Opposites must exist (good/evil, pleasure/pain, right/wrong)
3. Knowledge of good and evil
4. Power to choose

Pain as a Result of Laws Ordained by God

One of the laws God created and ordained is the law of gravity. "Gravity makes objects fall. Sometimes they fall on people and hurt them. Sometimes gravity makes people fall off mountains and out of windows. Sometimes gravity makes people slip on ice or sink under water. We could not live without gravity, but that means we have to live with the dangers it causes. Laws of nature treat everyone alike. They do not make exceptions for good people or for useful people. If a man enters a house where someone has a contagious disease, he runs the risk of catching that disease [unless the Lord protects the man supernaturally the way He protected Paul from the poisonous snake bite in Acts 28:3-5]. It makes no difference why he is in the house. He may be a doctor or a burglar; germs cannot tell the difference. . . . Laws of nature do not make exceptions for nice people. A bullet has no conscience; neither does a malignant tumor or an automobile gone out of control."[11] Christ taught this principle when he said, "[God] makes the sun rise on both good and bad people. And he sends rain for the ones who do right and for the ones who do wrong."[12] Thus, bad things are going to happen to good people, and good things are going to happen to bad people.

Pain as a Result of Opposition

For every right, there must be a wrong, and for every good, a bad. As a result of liberty, there will be joy and there will be pain. Since all people are given liberty, pain is inevitable for all. You may now be asking, "Why didn't God create a world where pain and suffering weren't necessary?" or "Wouldn't life be better if there were no adversity, pain, or opposition?"

Parable of the Two Schools

Given the two scenarios below, which of the two schools would you prefer to attend?

> **School No. 1.** You are required to study and work. Your grade is based on performance, so some will get As and others will fail. Only those who fulfill the requirements earn a degree. It is challenging and at times painful.

School No. 2. You must take tests, but all the tests are multiple choice. "C" is always the correct answer. You are required to answer "C" for each question, and everyone who takes the test receives a perfect score. Everyone receives a degree and graduates with a perfect 4.0 GPA. It is easy. It is free from work, pain, and struggle.

When I pose these two options at universities, the majority of the students choose School No. 2. I then ask, "How many would like to have surgery performed by a graduate of School No. 2?" Obviously, no hands are raised. If such a medical school existed, everyone would graduate with a perfect score and a medical degree. Graduates would be given the title of doctor, but the real purpose of learning the necessary skills of surgery would not have been achieved, and thus the diploma from such an institution would be worthless. Work, pain, struggle, and failure are part of the necessary education process to produce an individual with the skills of a surgeon.

When work, pain, and suffering are taken out of school, the purpose of school is defeated. Likewise, if God changed our current world to one where pain and suffering were eliminated, the purpose of life would be defeated. Life was not designed to be an existence of endless bliss. Life was designed to create greatness in each of us. "The command *Be ye perfect* is not idealistic gas. Nor is it a command to do the impossible. He is going to make us into creatures that can obey that command. . . . He will make the feeblest and filthiest of us into . . . a dazzling, radiant, immortal creature, pulsating all through with such energy and joy and wisdom and love as we cannot now imagine, a bright stainless mirror which reflects back to God perfectly (though, of course, on a smaller scale) His own boundless power and delight and good-ness. The process will be long and in parts very painful; but that is what we are in for. Nothing less. He meant what He said."[13]

Liberty gives us the power to think, choose, and act for our-selves. It is an eternal principle that has always existed and always will. Liberty creates opportunities for growth and joy, and at the same time creates failure, pain, and suffering. "Try to exclude the possibility of suffering which the order of nature and the exis-tence of free-wills involve, and you find that you have excluded life itself."[14] Liberty gives us the power to progress and improve our lives and the lives of those around us. Take away liberty, and you take away progression toward greatness.

Growth: Cause of Pain No. 2

We are all familiar with growing pains. Growth is a source of pain, but it is good pain. For example, when we lift weights or exercise, we experience pain. We have learned that this is a good pain, because from this pain come growth and improvement.

We often experience growing pains when we strive to reach the next level of prosperity. Sometimes the best people experi-ence great pain because they are ready to learn and grow. The Savior teaches in the parable of the Vine, "Every branch that bears fruit He prunes, that it may bear more fruit."[15] Pruning is the process of cutting off branches. Someone unfamiliar with the pruning process may think that the person pruning the vine is trying to punish, destroy, or kill the tree. While pruning does cause pain, its purpose is not to injure, harm, or punish. On the contrary, the pruning process eventually leads to a higher level of production.

Parable of the Renovated House

"Imagine yourself as a living house. God comes in to rebuild that house. At first perhaps, you can understand what He is doing. He is getting the drains right and stopping the leaks in the roof and so on: you knew that those jobs needed doing and so you are not surprised. But presently He starts knocking the house about in a way that hurts abominably and does not seem to make sense. What on earth is He up to? The explanation is that He is building quite a different house from the one you thought of— throwing out a new wing here, putting on an extra floor there, running up towers, making courtyards. You thought you were going to be made into a decent little cottage: but He is building a palace."[16] Jesus is the master carpenter, and he wants to build us into something great. As taught the apostle Paul, "God began doing a good work in you, and I am sure he will continue it until it is finished."[17]

Personal Choices/Sins: Cause of Pain No. 3

The power of choice brings with it great responsibility, as well as consequences. The consequences of our choices can lead to pain and suffering or joy. For example, if you choose to touch a hot stove, you will experience the pain of getting burned. The choice to smoke cigarettes can result in the pain of lung cancer. How do we avoid the pain of bad choices? One way is by following the commandments of God. God knows which choices result in pain and suffering and which result in joy. Learning and following the commandments of God will lead us to choices that will avoid the pain of personal sin and result in the joys of freedom and prosperity. We can eliminate future pain by learning from past mistakes and not repeating them.

Discipline

Many have asked the question, "Why would a loving God cause me pain because of a bad choice?" Just as loving parents discipline their children to lead them to a desirable result, so the pain of sin is God's way of disciplining us. He ultimately wants us to experience happiness, joy, and eternal life. As the apostle Paul taught, "God disciplines us for our good."[18] "For the Lord disciplines the one he loves."[19] And in the words of C. S. Lewis, "God whispers to us in our pleasure . . . and shouts in our pain."[20] You can stop the pain that results from personal sin at any time by ceasing the sin. You will only experience discipline and the pain of personal sin as long as you choose to.

Born with No Pain

Tony Dungy, former Indianapolis Colts head coach, has a son, Jordan, who was born with a rare condition that results in him feeling no pain. Coach Dungy shares the following in his book *Quiet Strength*: "Jordan is missing a gene, it turns out, and therefore doesn't feel pain the way other people do. Some experts think he might not feel any pain at all. For example, like most kids, Jordan loves cookies. . . . Jordan would reach right in [the oven] to pull out the piping hot cookie sheet with his bare hands. Then he would begin to eat the cookies without even realizing he was burning his hands and mouth in the process. Even a trip to the emergency room didn't help him understand he was injuring himself. . . . I think at one time or another every one of our children has gone running through the house at full tilt. Looking backward at a sibling in hot pursuit or waiting for a pass, they inevitably slam into a wall with the side of their head. They've all done it—once—and then, because of the pain, they're careful not to let it happen again. Jordan, on the other hand, does this kind of thing repeatedly and gets up smiling. Without the painful consequences, how is he to learn? . . . Before we had Jordan, I hadn't thought much about the way God uses pain to protect us from further negative consequences down the road. With Jordan, this has become obvious. Pain prompts us to change behavior that is destructive to ourselves or to others. Pain can be a highly effective instructor."[21]

Choices/Sins of Others: Cause of Pain No. 4

Choice must exist for us to have our God-given liberty. With this choice, people are able to help and hurt each other. If God stops people from using their choices in a bad way, He also takes away our liberty and ability to choose to use liberty in a good way. God did not cause or want Hitler to kill millions of innocent Jews. This pain was the result of Hitler choosing to use his God-given liberty for cruel and evil purposes.

My oldest brother works at a pharmacy that has been robbed several times. If one of these robbers were to choose to shoot my brother during the course of a robbery, my brother would experience the pain of a gunshot wound as a result of the robber's choices. The pain would not be my brother's fault, but he would experience pain nonetheless. Throughout our lives we all experience pain as the result of the choices and sins of others. The apostle Paul expressed this pain in a letter to the Corinthians: "Five times the Jews gave me thirty-nine lashes with a whip. Three times the Romans beat me with a big stick, and once my enemies stoned me. . . . During my many travels, I have been in danger from . . . robbers."[22]

Parable of the Wolf and the Shepherd

"The shepherd drives the wolf from the sheep's throat, for which the sheep thanks the shepherd as his liberator, while the wolf denounces him for the same act as the destroyer of liberty."[23] If you do good, the bad will denounce you as the wolf denounces the shepherd, but blessed are those who are persecuted for doing good. The Savior taught, "God blesses those people who are treated badly for doing right. . . . God will bless you when people insult you, mistreat you, and tell all kinds of evil lies about you."[24] "Rejoice, and be exceeding glad: for great is your reward in heaven: for so persecuted they the prophets which were before you."[25] It is "better to suffer for a good cause than live safely without one."[26] When people do bad things to us, we should respond with the courage to endure, and then rejoice, for the Lord will bless us with great rewards in heaven.

FOUR CAUSES OF PAIN ™	1. LIBERTY	2. GROWTH	3. PERSONAL CHOICES/ SINS	4. CHOICES/ SINS OF OTHERS
Why pain?	Opposition	Growing pains	Result of your negative action	Result of others' negative action
When does the pain stop?	Never	When higher level is attained	When we repent	Death
What is the proper response?	Courage	Faith/Good pain	Guilt/Bad pain	Rejoice/ Heavenly reward

Misapplying the Causes of Pain

To live is to experience pain. To survive and benefit from pain, we must learn why we experience pain and give meaning to the pain. When we experience pain, it can be helpful to identify which of the four reasons caused the pain. This will determine how we respond, interpret, and feel about the pain. "The sorest afflictions never appear intolerable, except when we see them in the wrong light."[27] Misapplying why pain has occurred will cause us to incorrectly respond to the pain. Many convince themselves that they are to blame and deserve the pain, even though it is often the result of liberty, growth, or the sins of others.

Misapplying Pain Caused by Liberty as Pain Caused by Sin

If we experience pain caused by liberty, but attribute the pain to a personal sin, we feel guilt for something we have not caused. A rabbi related the following story: a "middle-aged couple had one daughter, a bright nineteen-year-old, who was in her freshman year at an out-of-state college. One morning at breakfast, they received a phone call from the university infirmary. 'We have bad news for you. Your daughter collapsed while walking to class this morning. It seems a blood vessel burst in her brain. She died before we could do anything for her. We're terribly sorry. . . .' I went over to see them that same day. I entered their home feeling very inadequate, not knowing any word that could ease their pain. I anticipated anger, shock, grief but I didn't expect to hear the first words they said to me: 'You know, Rabbi, we didn't fast last Yom Kippur.' Why did they say that? Why did they assume that they were somehow responsible for this tragedy? . . . One of the ways in which people have tried to make sense of the world's suffering in every generation has been by assuming that we deserve what we get, that somehow our misfortunes come as punishment for our sins."[28]

This couple blamed themselves for their daughter's death

instead of identifying it as a possible result of liberty and natural laws, resulting in unnecessary guilt. Although innocent people can sometimes be hurt as a result of our sin, our loving God is not the one who hurts innocent people as a punishment for our sins. Would you punish your child for something your spouse did? As it was previously pointed out, the choices or sins of others is also one of the things that can causes innocent people to experience pain. But it is not the Lord who is punishing the innocent.

Not All Pain Is Beneficial

In the parable of the Vine, pruning led to growth and increased production. If the vine represents humanity, the cutting during the pruning process is for our benefit. This does not mean that all cutting is for our good, however. The mugger who stabs you with a knife is not pruning. The pain from the stab of the mugger is the result of liberty and sins of another. According to the Scripture, the victim who is a child of God can respond with courage and rejoicing in the midst of the persecution and pain, for great is your reward in heaven.[29] If we wrongly interpret the stabbing as a growing pain, we would interpret that we should respond with faith and view this pain as good. This would mean that God wanted you to get stabbed by the mugger so you could learn from the experience. While you can learn from and overcome the pain caused by the mugger, God did not want you to be stabbed. Would you stab one of your children with a knife so they could learn from the experience?

Misapplying Growth Pain and Pain from Personal Sin

At times we apply the good pain from growth to pain that is a result of personal sin. Misapplying the cause of pain in this way causes confusion and frustration, which can actually hinder growth. When you begin to dredge up sins you have committed to explain the pain you are experiencing, you will feel guilty and view the pain as a punishment. Many Christians are filled with guilt as the result of growth pains. How regrettable. They should be responding with faith and should rise to a higher level of discipleship. Instead, when this pain is misapplied, a person spirals downward with feelings of guilt and unworthiness. This thought process can also damage a person's relationship with God, for the person misunderstands His pruning as punishment instead of for growth and good.

Parable of the Weightlifter

If a weightlifter interpreted the growing pains he experienced as an injury, he would stop lifting and never grow. He would be misunderstanding the good pain of growth and would instead be filled with concern that he was injured. On the other hand, if the weightlifter did an exercise that caused injury but interpreted the pain as a growth pain, he would continue the exercise, resulting in more injury. Like the weightlifter, we too must be careful not to apply the pain from personal sin to growing pains. When we do this, we continue in a sin that results in a downward spiral when what we need to do is repent.

Conclusion: Courage

"Pain is inevitable, misery is optional. We cannot avoid pain in our lives, but we do have control over how we respond to that pain."[30] Courage is developing the ability to respond, endure, and, in some cases, overcome the pain, suffering, and hardships life can bring. It is not the ability to eliminate our fears but to act despite our fears. "Don't let the sensation of fear convince you that you're too weak to have courage. Fear is the opportunity for courage, not proof of cowardice."[31]

We are not left to deal with the challenges of life alone. We can call upon God, and He will assist us. The Savior extends to each of us this invitation: "Come unto me, all ye that labour and are heavy laden, and I will give you rest. Take my yoke upon you, and learn of me; for I am meek and lowly in heart: and ye shall find rest unto your souls. For my yoke is easy, and my burden is light."[32] The goal is not to eliminate pain but to properly respond to pain. "Be strong and courageous. Do not be afraid or discouraged."[33]

Paul endured well the pain he suffered. Shortly before his death Paul wrote to Timothy from his prison cell in Rome: "I have fought a good fight, I have finished my course, I have kept the faith: Henceforth there is laid up for me a crown of righteousness, which the Lord, the righteous judge, shall give me at that day: and not to me only, but unto all them also that love his appearing."[34] We need to have the courage to endure life's pain and face our fears so that the Savior may say to each of us, "Well done, thou good and faithful servant: thou hast been faithful over a few things, I will make thee ruler over many things: enter thou into the joy of thy lord."[35]

CHAPTER 8

THE PARADOX OF CHOICE

*"They answered him [Jesus], We . . . were never in
bondage to any man: how sayest thou, Ye shall be made
free? Jesus answered them, Verily, verily, I say unto you,
Whosoever committeth sin is the servant of sin."*
—John 8:33–34, King James Version

We have all heard someone describe freedom as follows:
"Freedom is doing whatever I want. No one can tell me what to
do. God's commandments are restrictive. I am not in bondage to
any man." They falsely believe that not obeying God's commandments gives them more freedom, when the exact opposite
is actually the case. For example, two people are looking for a
place to swim when they come upon a sign that reads, "Danger!
Whirlpool—No Swimming Allowed." Both of these people have
the power to choose whether to swim here. One swimmer chooses to enter the water and is sucked in. As a result of his choice,
he is now in bondage to the whirlpool. The other person chooses not to enter the water and as a result has the freedom to find
another place to swim. The correct use of our power to choose
results in more choices. The misuse results in fewer choices. Each
time we make a choice; we either gain more freedom as a result
of our increased choices or digress toward bondage as the result
of our diminished choices.

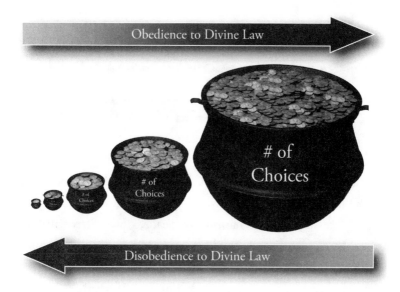

The laws of God are not restrictive, but are a road map to joy. The violation of these laws is not freedom but bondage, pain, and misery. As taught the Savior, "Whoever commits sin is a slave of sin."[1] Those who know and live the commands of God enjoy freedom, joy, and prosperity. Thus, obedience to the laws of God is freedom.

Divine Law—Choice and Consequence

Each divine law creates a choice to obey or disobey. With each choice comes a divinely appointed consequence. No amount of rationalizing or complaining alters the consequence. If you pick up one end of a stick (choice), you also pick up the other end of the stick (consequence of that choice).

Many of the choices we make can lead to either obeying or disobeying a divine law. As we obey divine laws we move to a more successful state of happiness, peace, power, freedom, and prosperity. As we disobey the laws, we move to a state of sadness, weakness, bondage, and misery. Each moment we are progressing toward one of these two states. This gift of choice is like fire: if properly used, it creates warmth and life; if improperly used, it can burn or even kill. The Bible declares, "Behold, I set before you this day a blessing and a curse; A blessing, if ye obey the commandments of the LORD your God . . . And a curse, if ye will not obey the commandments of the LORD your God."[2]

Farm Metaphor

On a farm, you reap what you sow. If you plant corn, you harvest corn. You cannot plant corn and harvest watermelon. Similarly we reap what we sow in life. Our choices are the seeds, and the consequences the harvest. At times we may attempt to choose the consequences of our choices or misunderstand what the consequence of a choice will be. We might want to eat ten thousand calories a day and not gain weight. We might want to smoke cigarettes but not get lung cancer. We want to violate divine laws and still have freedom and prosperity. This is as foolish as a farmer planting corn and expecting to harvest watermelon. Some might also expect financial abundance but learn nothing regarding the laws of wealth. This is as silly as a farmer not planting and expecting a great harvest.

The Prison Lecture

While speaking at a prison to a group of inmates, I asked for a volunteer from the inmates to describe his dream life. After a long pause and some prodding, one of the inmates began to speak. I was rather surprised by his vivid description of a successful career, a beautiful home, and a loving, happy family.

I then asked, "Why are you in prison?"

The inmate responded, "For drugs."

I then asked if drugs would take him away from or toward the dream life he described. I will never forget his response: "I can have both."

I replied by saying, "What would happen if you touched a hot stove with your bare hand?"

The inmate replied, "I would get burned."

I continued, "What if you don't want to get burned? Can you just choose to touch a hot stove and not get burned?" He, of course, answered no.

I then taught that we can choose whether or not to touch a hot stove, but we cannot decide whether or not we get burned. We can choose our actions, but we cannot choose the consequences of our choices. Getting burned is a natural consequence of touching a hot stove, just like a prison sentence is the consequence of being involved with illegal drugs.

To this the inmate replied, "I am in prison, have no money, am divorced, and rarely see my kids. If you're so smart, how do I change this?"

I answered, "You need to learn and live divine laws."

The inmate replied, "What do you mean?"

I continued, "Our lives are governed by divine laws, such as gravity. A child, though ignorant of the law, will still fall if he jumps off a ledge and will still get burned if he touches a hot stove. The divine laws that govern wealth, health, relationships, and our spirits are as clear and as binding as those that govern the earth, such as gravity. Regardless of whether we know or understand divine laws, they always operate the same. Our success or failure, our happiness or unhappiness, depends on our knowledge and application of these laws in our lives."

The inmate then asked, "So why are some people rich and some poor?"

I replied, "Why are some people physically fit and others overweight?" I explained that people's health differs because they have made different choices. Consider someone with a lot of money who is overweight. This person has learned to live financial laws but does not live the laws of health. Something similar could be said about someone who is in great shape and is poor. That person has learned to live the laws of health but not the laws of wealth. The great news is that you can be successful in all areas of your life by living the divine laws related to each area.

The inmate then asked, "You are obviously successful. Can I achieve success?"

In response, I asked the inmate to climb on the table he was sitting at, and I climbed onto the table at the front of the room. I then said, "On the count of three, jump off the table. One, two, three." We both jumped off the table and hit the floor. I continued teaching that the law of gravity affected both of us the same, regardless of age, gender, race, or upbringing. This is also true of the laws of success. They are the same now as they were in the past and will be the same in the future. Our knowledge about these laws may fluctuate, but their principles and application will never change. Anyone can be successful, because anyone can learn and follow the laws of success.

God has blessed all people with liberty. This great freedom of choice is what determines who we will become. All people are born equal but become unequal as they make decisions. Every person chooses to obey laws differently. One may choose to play softball while another chooses to build a business. One may choose to turn on the television while another chooses to read books. One may choose to play golf on her day off while another chooses to spend time with his family. One person chooses to listen to the radio on the way to work, and another person chooses to listen to positive audio books. We are born equal, yet years later live diversely, all because we chose to live divine laws differently. It is really very simple: following divine laws results in positive outcomes.

Years later I was at a chamber of commerce meeting and recognized the inmate I had spoken with at the prison. He approached me and said, "Thank you so much for visiting me in prison; your message changed my life. I always wondered why some men had great lives while mine was miserable. I saw people with successful careers, beautiful homes, and happy families and wondered why my life was just the opposite. Once I learned that there were divine laws to success, my heart was filled with hope and peace. I realized that all I had to do was learn these laws and then have courage, discipline, and the guts to obey them. Once I realized this, I knew that I would one day live my dreams, have a successful career, and be a hero to my wife and children. It has been a long road, but I have transformed my life from one of bondage and misery to one of freedom and prosperity."[3]

CHAPTER 9

THE PARADOX OF FORGIVENESS

*"Ye have heard that it hath been said, An eye for an eye,
and a tooth for a tooth: But I say unto you, That ye resist
not evil: but whosoever shall smite thee on thy right
cheek, turn to him the other also. And if any man will
sue thee at the law, and take away thy coat, let him have
thy cloke also."*
—Matthew 5:38–40, King James Version

The world and a natural person will often respond with revenge
and anger toward those who harm them. For example, several
years ago, one of the speakers for one of my companies was invited to speak at a large convention in New York City. One of the
speakers at the convention was Donald Trump. During his
speech, Trump talked about his "F off list," although he did not
abbreviate the swear word. He told the audience that every time
someone did something wrong to him, he put them on his "F off
list," and if that person ever calls him or his office, the reception-
ist would tell the person to F off and then slam down the phone.
He then went on to tell a story of a man who crossed him and
how he was able to get revenge, and when the man called him he
told him to F off and slammed down the phone. The story was
a big turnoff to me, but the audience had a much different reaction: they rose to their feet and gave him a standing ovation. It
is disappointing to me that such behavior would be a model for
anyone to follow.

The Savior has given us a much different model to follow. Jesus Christ's life exemplified the attitude of forgiveness we should seek to emulate. In the final hours of His life, Christ was betrayed by Judas, His friend and apostle.[1] He was unjustly arrested[2] and had false witnesses testify against Him.[3] "They spit in His Face,"[4] "beat Him,"[5] and "slapped Him."[6] "They tied Him up"[7] and "stripped off [His] clothes."[8] They gave Him a severe beating with a whip containing embedded pieces of bone and metal.[9] They placed a "crown of thorns . . . upon His head"[10] and "mocked Him."[11] They then "spit upon Him"[12] again. They then required Him to carry the cross upon which He was to suffer.[13] When Christ arrived at Golgotha, they nailed His hands, wrists, and feet to the cross to be crucified.[14] The New Testament records seven statements of Christ from the cross. After all the hatred, evil, punishment, and pain Christ endured, His first words from the cross were, "Father, forgive them; for they know not what they do."[15]

The Savior perfectly exemplified his words, "Ye have heard that it hath been said, Thou shalt love thy neighbour, and hate thine enemy. But I say unto you, Love your enemies, bless them that curse you, do good to them that hate you, and pray for them which despitefully use you, and persecute you."[16] A church leader taught, "A spirit of forgiveness and an attitude of love and compassion toward those who may have wronged us is the very essence of the gospel of Jesus Christ."

Return Good for Evil

We have a natural tendency to treat others as they treat us. Returning good for good and evil for evil is known as the law of reciprocity. This law results in either the improvement or decline of a relationship. For example, if someone is unkind to you, you respond naturally by being unkind to them. Your unkindness leads to their continued unkindness to you, and suddenly you have produced a cyclical relationship with each person returning more and more unkindness. The end result is a very unproductive and destructive relationship.

The law of reciprocity can also work in a positive direction. For example, if you show someone kindness and love, they respond naturally with kindness, which causes you to respond with even more kindness and love. This cyclical effect returns more and more kindness and love, producing a more meaningful and loving relationship. The Lord's command to return love for hate, concern and prayer for persecution, and blessing for cursing enables us to reverse the negative cycle of reciprocity.

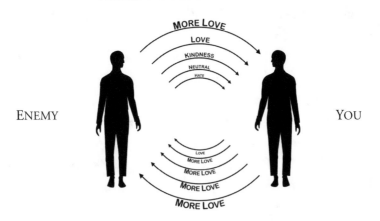

REVERSING THE RECIPROCITY CYCLE

The Accidental Gift

My wife, Paula, is one of the most loving, friendly, outgoing people I know. A few years ago she was in a car accident. She was stopped at a traffic light when a person three cars back failed to stop, causing a four-car accident. My wife did not have her insurance information with her. When I arrived with the insurance information, the police were taking statements and information. The drivers of the other damaged cars were upset and angry, but Paula was happy and making friends. Paula went up to the driver responsible for the accident and gave her a hug and said, "You need a present." My wife then gave her two tickets to a local college football game taking place on the upcoming Saturday. The girl said in shock, "I damaged your car and caused you and your baby a great deal of stress, and you're giving me a present?"

Gandhi Returns Love for Hatred and Frees a Nation

Gandhi wrote, "It is easy enough to be friendly to one's friends. But to befriend the one who regards himself as your enemy is the sign of true religion." Gandhi fought for equal rights, fair treatment, and independence from British domination for the Indian people, but his was not the traditional fight. Gandhi sought to overcome their exploitation "by returning love for hatred, and respect for contempt."[17] Gandhi had learned, "When one person hates another, it is the hater who falls ill—physically, emotionally, spiritually. When he loves, it is he who becomes whole. Hatred kills. Love heals."[18] He also discovered that "an eye for an eye only ends up making the whole world blind."[19] Gandhi challenged the people, "Do not resort to violence even if it seems at first to promise success; it can only contradict your purpose. Use the means of love and respect even if the result seems far off or uncertain. . . . If we can adhere [to these principles], India's freedom is assured. . . . I hold myself to be incapable of hating any being on earth. . . . But I can and do hate evil wherever it exists. I hate the system of government that the British people have set up in India. I hate the ruthless exploitation of India. . . . I do not hate the domineering Englishmen. . . . I seek to reform them in all the loving ways that are open to me. My noncooperation has its roots not in hatred, but in love."[20]

When scholar J. B. Kripalani first heard Gandhi talk about fighting for independence with love and respect instead of violence, he walked up to Gandhi and told him, "Mr. Gandhi . . . you know nothing at all about history. Never has a nation been able to free itself without violence." Gandhi smiled and replied, "You know nothing about history. The first thing you have to learn about history is that because something has not taken place in the past that does not mean it cannot take place in the future."[21]

As a result of Gandhi's refusal to obey unjust laws, he was imprisoned several times, spending six and a half years of his life in prison. During one of his stays in prison he made a pair of sandals for the man responsible for his imprisonment, Field General Jan Smuts. Many years later Smuts wrote of Gandhi, "In jail he prepared for me a pair of sandals. I have worn them for many a summer, though I feel that I am not worthy to stand in the shoes of so great a man."[22] Late in his life Gandhi said of General Smuts, "He started with being my bitterest opponent and critic. Today he is my warmest friend."

Returning Love for Hatred during World War II

At the conclusion of World War II, the survivors in the concentration camps were freed. Many prisoners were weak and filled with anger. In one of the camps, the American soldiers observed a man who appeared to be strong, happy, and peaceful. His eyes were bright and his energy unwavering. The soldiers assumed he had recently been imprisoned or had not suffered as the other prisoners had. As this prisoner was questioned, it was learned that "for six years he had lived on the same starvation diet, slept in the same airless and disease-ridden barracks as everyone else, but without the least physical or mental deterioration." Explaining what made the difference, he related the following: "We lived in the Jewish section of Warsaw [capital of Poland], my wife, two daughters, and our three little boys. When the Germans reached our street they lined everyone against a wall and opened up with machine guns. I begged to be allowed to die with my family, but because I spoke German they put me in a work group. I had to decide right then whether to let myself hate the soldiers who had done this. It was an easy decision, really. I was a lawyer. In my practice I had seen too often what hate could do to people's minds and bodies. Hate had just killed the six people who mattered most to me in the world. I decided then that I would spend the rest of my life—whether it was a few days or many years—loving every person I came in contact with."[23]

Forgiving

One of my mentors shared the following story about a group of teenagers who went for a picnic in the desert outside of Phoenix. While they were playing, a rattlesnake bit one of the girls on the ankle. The girl and her friends pursued the snake and after about twenty minutes were able to find the snake and kill it. Once the snake was destroyed, they headed to the emergency room. A couple days later her foot and leg had swollen almost beyond recognition. The tissues in her limb had been destroyed by the poison, and a few days later it was found her leg would have to be amputated below the knee. It was a senseless sacrifice, the price of revenge. How much better it would have been if after the young woman had been bitten, there had been an extraction of the venom.

It is difficult for us to forgive those who have injured us, but dwelling on the evil done to us becomes an erosive and destructive poison. Nelson Mandela wrote, "Resentment is like drinking poison and then hoping it will kill your enemies."

In January 2001 I had completed a lecture at a university in which I talked about working to prevent child abuse. I was talking to my mom on the phone about the presentation, and we began talking about the abuse of my childhood. During our conversion my mom asked me, "Have you forgiven him?" I said, "Yes, I have. I forgave him years ago." Tears came to my eyes and pain filled my heart as my mom described the pain and struggles she experienced as a result of her son being abused by someone she trusted—someone she loved. My mom then said, "I can't forgive him." Although she is one of the kindest, most caring Christians in the world, she could not forgive him for hurting her son.

Nearly five years later, in the fall of 2005, I got a call from my mom to tell me she had forgiven the relative responsible for the abuse. She related the experience to me over the phone, and I asked that she write it down and send it to me. My mother wrote the following:

> I had known for a long time that I needed to forgive Henry [name has been changed] for sexually

abusing my son. I kept postponing it because I felt that if I forgave him, then I would be condoning it somehow. One morning I felt prompted that I needed to go through the process of forgiving him and letting go of all the hurt and anger.

I felt prompted to go to the cemetery where he was buried and prayed for the help of the Lord to take away this burden that I had carried with me for so many years. I began to share my feelings and told the Lord that I was really ready to let it all go. I knew that holding onto it was keeping me from progressing spiritually.

I went to the cemetery where Henry was buried. After spending some time at Henry's gravesite, I felt prompted to go and run around the track at the high school. I thought that was strange because I am definitely not a runner. I usually walk for exercise but cannot run very far. As I was thinking about this, the story of the leper Naaman who went to Elisha to be healed came to my mind. Elisha told Naaman, "Go and wash in the Jordan seven times, and your flesh shall be restored to you, and you shall be clean."[24] But Naaman rejected the counsel, for he expected a mighty miracle. "Naaman became furious"[25] "and went away in a rage."[26] Naaman's servant then spoke to him, saying, "If the prophet had told you to do something great, would you not have done it? How much more then, when he says to you, 'Wash, and be clean'?"[27] Naaman then went and washed seven times in the Jordan and was healed.

I figured I better follow the prompting, so I went to the track and thought maybe I could run around one time. As I began to run and my heart began to beat faster, I felt a burden being lifted off of me. My heart felt good, and I knew that the Lord was blessing me with the ability to forgive. I then felt a great remorse for being unforgiving for so long. I asked the Lord for forgiveness for not acting upon this sooner. I felt a peace come over me that was so wonderful, and I actually felt changed physically and spiritually. I walked around the track another lap and said a prayer of gratitude to the Heavenly Father for His great love for me and expressed appreciation for the power of the atonement of Jesus Christ, which heals what we cannot heal on our own. Just as Naaman's leprosy was healed by washing in the Jordan, my hurt and anger were healed by forgiving.

Leonardo da Vinci and Forgiveness[28]

Leonardo da Vinci worked on painting *The Last Supper* for three years from 1495 to 1498. The painting was commissioned by the Duke Lodovico Sforza for the dining hall of the convent of Santa Maria delle Grazie, in Milan, Italy. As the painting neared completion there were still two heads that were unfinished: Christ and Judas. Da Vinci had not yet found an acceptable model for Judas. For the image of Christ, he knew he needed inspiration to depict the heavenly divinity of the Master.

Milanese novelist Bandello, who often visited da Vinci while he worked on *The Last Supper*, related the following, "I have often seen him come very early and watched him mount the scaffolding—because *The Last Supper* is somewhat high above the floor—and then he would not put down his brush from sunrise till the night set in, yes, he forgot eating and drinking, and painted without ceasing. Then two, three or four days would pass without him doing anything, and yet he spent hours before the picture, lost in contemplation, examining, comparing, and gauging his figures."

The days of no painting by da Vinci offended one of the priors (ruling magistrate), and receiving no answer to his complaint from da Vinci, this dignitary who was accustomed to see workmen do their daily task went to the duke and laid complaints against the idle painter. The duke called in da Vinci and admonished him to paint, but told him he only did so to please the prior. Da Vinci got angry, and knowing that Duke Lodovico was a sensible and intelligent man, he explained to him that great minds accomplish all the more, the less they appear to work, because their intellect invents and shapes the ideals that their hands afterward delineate and work out. He added that he still wanted two heads for his picture: that of Christ, for which he could not find a model on earth, and that of Judas, because he could not devise a countenance to represent the face of him who, after all the benefits he had received, shamefully betrays his Lord, the Creator of the world. Da Vinci then said that he no longer need to look for a model for Judas for he would use the head of the prior for his model. The duke smiled, and the prior feared he would be known as the face of the traitor Judas.

Da Vinci proceeded to paint the head of Judas as the prior who had reported his idleness to the duke. Once he completed the head of Judas, da Vinci began to work on the face of the Savior. Da Vinci made several attempts to portray the face of the Master, but each attempt left him with feelings of despair. He was unable to receive the inspiration he sought and needed to portray the face of the Redeemer of the World. Da Vinci then wiped off the face of Judas and sought out the prior to ask for his forgiveness. It is recorded that on the night following his reconciliation with the prior, da Vinci saw Christ in a vision. Da Vinci saw the face of Christ more vividly than he ever saw it in his supreme moments of exalted inspiration, and so lasting was the impression that he was able on the next day to paint the face of Christ we see in *The Last Supper* today.

Conclusion

Blame and grudges keep wounds open and allow the wrongs of others to control our lives. Forgiveness is not easy, but it is the balm that heals our wounds and frees us to choose our destiny.

CHAPTER 10

THE PARADOX OF WEALTH

"There is one who makes himself rich, yet has nothing;
And one who makes himself poor, yet has great riches."
—Proverbs 13:7, New King James Version

The son of a business executive shared this story: "I grew up in a brutal business environment. My father worked as the chief executive for one of the richest men in the world, Howard Hughes, and that world turned many lives upside down. I witnessed firsthand greed, deception, power struggles, and destruction of souls all for the sake of money. But perhaps what influenced me most is what I had seen in Mr. Hughes himself. For many years on Christmas Eve or Easter Sunday, this annual ritual was not what it appeared to be; Mr. Hughes invited my father to his home. When my father arrived, Mr. Hughes would simply say, 'Bill, I just wanted to talk.' Then after a couple of hours of friendly conversation he would say, 'It's Christmas. You better get back to your family.' And I remember thinking to myself: 'With all the money, with all the power, all the accomplishments, and even all the good he has done, he is both lonely and alone.'"[1]

This story illustrates the paradox "There is one who makes himself rich, yet has nothing."[2] It is also true that one may have nothing, yet still have everything.

What Makes Money Good or Bad?

"A hammer is a tool. If one learns to use it well, a house can be built. If one doesn't use it well there will be many broken and bruised and very painful thumbs."

—Lloyd Porter

Many people believe that money is bad. The truth is that money, in and of itself, is not good or evil. You could put a billion dollars into a room, and it would never do anything good or bad. Money is good or bad depending on the person who possesses it. A person's personality and character are magnified by their use of money. C. S. Lewis taught, "Surely what a man does when he is taken off his guard is the best evidence for what sort of a man he is? Surely what pops out before the man has time to put on a disguise is the truth? If there are rats in a cellar you are most likely to see them if you go in very suddenly. But the suddenness does not create the rats; it only prevents them from hiding. In the same way the suddenness of the provocation does not make me an ill-tempered man: it only shows me what an ill-tempered man I am."[3] Likewise, money does not create greed, pride, or any other negative trait. It simply magnifies a person's character to a point where their strengths and weakness cannot be hidden. Thus, it is not virtuous to be poor, nor is it virtuous to be rich. It is virtuous to be virtuous.

Money is a tool that expands our ability to do both good and evil in the world. For example, the invention of the printing press has enabled us to mass produce positive materials such as the Bible. On the other hand, it has also increased the availability of pornography. The printing press by itself is neither good nor evil. Good people utilize the printing press to improve society. Bad people use the printing press to degrade society. This same analogy can be applied to the television, radio, telephone, Internet, and other advances in technology—with each advance, our ability to do both good and evil increases. Money, like all tools, is good or bad as a result of how it is utilized.

If having wealth increases our power to do evil, is the solution to not be rich? Of course not. This solution would be as silly as doing away with the printing press and Internet because of pornography. Some are concerned about obtaining wealth, fearing that it will corrupt them. This would be similar to saying, "I am not going to get married, because I don't want to commit adultery." While it is true that if no one were to get married, there would not be any adultery, the solution to adultery is not to eliminate marriage. The solution is for people to be faithful to their marriage covenants. The same applies to money. The solution is not to eliminate wealth and abundance but for people to faithfully fulfill their financial stewardships. It is not the amount of money we have but our attitudes toward it and use of it that makes it good or bad.

Money is a Bad Tool When . . .	Money is a Good Tool When . . .
1. A person trusts in money	1. A person trusts in God
2. A person puts money first	2. A person puts God first
3. It is used for oneself	3. It is used for God
4. A person is greedy and selfish	4. A person is charitable or shares freely
5. It is earned by immoral means	5. It is earned by honorable means
6. It is viewed as "my money"	6. It is viewed as "God's money"

1. Trust in Money vs. Trust in God

One source often used to support the myth that money is bad comes from misunderstanding the following New Testament story: "And a certain ruler asked him, saying, Good Master, what shall I do to inherit eternal life? And Jesus said unto him . . . sell all that thou hast, and distribute unto the poor, and thou shalt have treasure in heaven: and come, follow me. And when he heard this, he was very sorrowful: for he was very rich. And when Jesus saw that he was very sorrowful, he said, How hardly shall they that have riches enter into the kingdom of God! For it is easier for a camel to go through a needle's eye, than for a rich man to enter into the kingdom of God."[4]

Many have misunderstood this, believing that it is hard for rich people to go to heaven. This is not the case. In answer to the apostles' question, "Who then can be saved?"[5] Jesus clarifies what He meant by saying, "How hard is it for them that *trust in riches* to enter into the kingdom of God!"[6] Christ was not teaching that riches are bad but that trusting in riches is bad. The Bible also says, "Blessed be ye poor, for yours is the kingdom of God."[7] Does this mean people are going to heaven simply because they are poor? Of course not. To say it is hard for the rich to go to heaven is as silly as saying it is easy for the poor to go to heaven. Our admittance to heaven is not dependent on our net worth. Whether you are rich or poor, you must "trust . . . in the living God"[8] to go to heaven.

God is not going to keep anyone out of heaven because he or she had wealth. The Bible teaches, "Thou shalt remember the Lord thy God: for it is he that giveth thee power to get wealth."[9] Many people of God have been rich. The Bible tells us Abraham "was very rich in cattle, silver, and in gold,"[10] and that Isaac "became rich, and gained more and more until he became very wealthy. He had possessions of flocks and herds and many servants."[11] The Bible also tells us of one of Jesus' rich disciples, saying, "A rich man of Arimathaea, named Joseph, who also himself was Jesus' disciple."[12] Riches are a righteous desire when we trust in God.

2. Money First vs. God First

Near the end of my junior year in college, I received two job offers. Both required one-year commitments and were full-time during the summer and part-time positions during the school year. The first job was to write and teach about Christ-centered leadership at the university I was attending. The second was a corporate management and training job, which paid $48,000 more per year than the offer from the university. My family and friends suggested I would be crazy not to take the higher-paying job. If the decision was only based on money, the corporate job would have been an easy choice.

I went to the Lord in prayer and asked which job He would like me to take. The answer came to take the job with the university and the scripture came to my mind, "Seek ye first the kingdom of God, and his righteousness; and all these things [earthly possessions] shall be added unto you."[13] Exercising faith and an attitude of "What would God have me do?" I took the job at the university.

Whether we realize it or not, we each have a top priority in our life. Some of the things people center their lives around are God, family, money, work, possessions, friends, church, and self. What we make our top priority affects how we live, act, and see the world. True prosperity, success, and happiness come when God is at the center of our lives—when He is our number-one priority. The Lord said, "If any man come to me, and hate not his father, and mother, and wife, and children, and brethren and sisters, yea, and his own life also, he cannot be my disciple."[14] Is the Lord teaching us that families are bad and that anyone who loves his family cannot be His disciple? Of course not. In this scripture, the Lord teaches an important principle: we must always put God first. "If you let important responsibilities like family, work, and money become the center of your attention instead of God—if you concentrate on them too much or too long—you will soon lose your ability to relate to God, and life will become meaningless."[15]

Our families, our jobs, and the numerous pleasures of life are all good things when we put God first. However, if anything other than God becomes the center of our lives, we have lost the focus that will bring us true happiness, joy, and prosperity. Having a family is good unless it replaces God as the center of our lives. Money is good unless it replaces God as our number-one priority. To say that having money is bad would be as foolish as saying having a family, attending church, or working are bad. The scriptures do not say, "Money is the root of all evil." They say, "The *love* of money is the root of all evil."[16] When you put money first—when it becomes your center and motive for what you do—then money will produce negative results. When God is at the center of our lives, money is good and desirable. When we put God first, wealth will not have a negative impact on us.

3. Do It for Yourself vs. Do It for God

Many have compartmentalized God and money as two unrelated portions of their lives, believing that God and money are unrelated and not to be discussed in the same context. I have seen this in my businesses as good Christian employees are uncomfortable when I start company meetings with prayer or seek divine guidance for answers to business problems and challenges. I also receive complaints when I give sermons on topics related to money, receiving such comments as, "We should not talk about money at church." "The relative absence of sermons about money—which the Bible mentions several thousand times—is one of the more stunning omissions in American religion. . . . There has long been a taboo on talking candidly about money."[17]

Many have taken God out of their jobs and the portions of their lives related to money. The truly prosperous have learned to include God in all their actions, even those involving money. In the eyes of God, the world is not compartmentalized into temporal and spiritual, for all things are spiritual to Him. "There is one God and Father of everything. He rules everything and is everywhere and is in everything."[18]

We must learn to involve God in everything we do. The Lord has commanded us to work and provide for ourselves and our families. The Lord said to Adam, "In the sweat of your face you shall eat bread, till you return to the ground."[19] The apostle Paul taught, "But if any provide not for his own, and specially for those of his own house, he hath denied the faith, and is worse than an infidel."[20] We should do all our work for the love of God, and He will guide and strengthen our performance.

A seventeenth-century cook learned to do his work not for himself but for God. He began each day with this prayer, "'O my God, since Thou art with me, and I must now, in obedience to Thy commands, apply my mind to these outward things, I beseech Thee to grant me the grace to continue in Thy presence; and to this end do Thou prosper me with Thy assistance.' . . . In his business in the kitchen (to which he had naturally a great aversion), having accustomed himself to do everything there for the love of God, and with prayer . . . to do his work well, he found everything easy, during fifteen years that he had been employed there."[21] He said of his work as a cook, "'The time of business does not with me differ from the time of prayer; and in the noise and clutter of my kitchen, while several persons are at the same time calling for different things, I possess God in as great tranquility as if I were upon my knees at the blessed sacrament.' . . . The foundation of the spiritual life in him had been . . . that he might perform all his actions for the love of God."[22]

As Sam Walton, founder of Wal-Mart, neared the end of his life, dying of cancer, he reflected on his life's work and wondered if he should have spent his time doing something else to improve the world. He wondered if he made the right choice to invest so much time in building Wal-Mart. After much thought, he concluded that his work at Wal-Mart was his life ministry—that through his retail business, he was able to improve and bless the lives of others. He wrote, "Preachers are put here to minister to our souls; doctors to heal our diseases; teachers to open up our minds; and so on. Everybody has their role to play. The thing is, I am absolutely convinced that the only way we can improve one another's quality of life . . . is through what we call free enterprise—practiced correctly and morally. . . . We've improved the standard of living of our customers, whom we've saved billions of dollars, and of our associates, who have been able to share profits. . . . Those companies out there who aren't . . . focusing on the customers' interest are just going to get lost. . . . Those who get greedy are going to be left in the dust. [Business must] benefit the workers, the stockholders, the communities, and of course, management, which must adopt a philosophy of servant leadership."[23]

"Today we often feel we must 'get away' from our daily routine in order to worship God, but . . . worship [is] not an event to attend, but a perpetual attitude."[24] Our jobs and businesses should be driven by service and viewed as an ever-unfolding and expanding ministry. What we do, we should do for God. The apostle Paul taught, "Do your work heartily, as for the Lord rather than for men."[25]

4. Greed/Selfishness vs. Charity/Sharing

Greed and selfishness are things each of us must guard against. The Savior has warned us, saying, "Watch out! Be on your guard against all kinds of greed."[26] Greed is an unsatisfiable desire. The Bible teaches that "greedy dogs . . . can never have enough,"[27] and "Whoever loves money never has money enough; whoever loves wealth is never satisfied with his income."[28] No matter how much a greedy person has, it will never be enough.

The Savior gave two parables warning against greed and the hoarding of our possessions: "And he told them this parable: The ground of a certain rich man produced a good crop. He thought to himself, 'What shall I do? I have no place to store my crops.' Then he said, 'This is what I'll do. I will tear down my barns and build bigger ones, and there I will store all my grain and my goods. . . . But God said to him, 'You fool! This very night your life will be demanded from you.'"[29] The Savior also told the following parable. "There was a rich man who was dressed in purple and fine linen and lived in luxury every day. At his gate was laid a beggar named Lazarus, covered with sores and longing to eat what fell from the rich man's table. . . . The time came when the beggar died and the angels carried him to Abraham's side. The rich man also died [and was taken to hell]."[30]

Is the message from these parables that rich people go to hell?

Of course not. If this was the case, Abraham would not have been in heaven, for he was a very rich man on earth. The rich man was sent to hell not for being rich, but for denying the beggar food and not giving of his money. The message is not that riches are bad, but that greed and selfishness are bad. Wealth and riches are good when they are used to build the kingdom of God and care for His children. Wealth allows you to cloth the naked, feed the hungry, and nourish the sick. As disciples of Christ, we should be filled with a love that will motivate us to use our riches to care for the needs of other people.

5. Achieved by Immoral Means vs. Achieved by Honorable Means

If we violate a law of God to obtain money, that money is bad. Money obtained by theft, bribery, false advertising, excessive charges, exploiting employees,[31] or from the sale of gambling, pornography, harmful drugs, or other sinful practices is what the Bible calls filthy lucre.[32] Money acquired through the violation of divine law is never worth its cost. The Savior taught, "For what is a man profited, if he shall gain the whole world, and lose his own soul? Or what shall a man give in exchange for his soul?"[33]

The Lord expects us to be honest and treat others fairly in our work and financial duties. The Bible teaches that as we follow the laws of God, we will be blessed. "Do not let this Book of the Law depart from your mouth; meditate on it day and night, so that you may be careful to do everything written in it. Then you will be prosperous and successful."[34]

6. My Money vs. God's Money

"Always remember that your lives, your ability, the food you eat, the water you drink, the clothes you wear, the earth you tread, the air you breathe, are all the Lord's. . . . Then, whether you are rich or poor will make no difference. . . . You will look upon yourselves as stewards, and if you have a hundred dollars in your hands, you will say, this is the Lord's, and if He wants it, He can have it. If you have a million dollars, you will feel the same. And where people have this feeling, riches cannot hurt them."[35]

"Is it Mine?" or "Is It God's?"

The first home my wife and I purchased was in the mountains. Although we loved our home, our backyard was an undeveloped mountainside, a potentially dangerous play area for our children. To solve this problem, we decided to build two rock retaining walls on the mountain to create a large grass playing field below our home. I called a friend in the landscaping business for a bid on the cost of the project. He estimated it would cost forty thousand dollars. Our friend agreed to start on the project the following week, so we wrote him a check for twenty thousand dollars to cover the expenses of the subcontractors to build the retaining walls.

As it turned out, our friend was experiencing financial difficulties and spent the twenty thousand dollars on items other than the renovating of our yard. He hid this from my wife and me for months, continually telling us he would start in a few weeks. Since we loved and trusted him, we never suspected him of dishonesty. When we finally discovered the truth, the summer was over, our yard was still undeveloped, and we were out twenty thousand dollars. It was frustrating for us, and we were unsure of the most appropriate way to handle the situation.

As I pondered how to respond, the Lord's Prayer came to my mind: "Give us this day our daily bread."[36] Reading this passage helped me realize that everything we have comes from God, so nothing that we have is really ours. God gave me the twenty thousand dollars, so the money our friend had taken was not mine, but the Lord's.

The prayer continues, "Forgive us our debts, as we forgive our debtors. . . . For if ye forgive men their trespasses, your heavenly Father will also forgive you: But if ye forgive not men their trespasses, neither will your Father forgive your trespasses."[37] I also read the parable the Savior taught in answer to Peter's questions about how often he should forgive. In this parable, a servant was forgiven by the king a debt of 10,000 talents (60 million pence, approximately $3 billion today).[38] "But the same servant went out, and found one of his fellowservants, which owed him an hundred pence (approximately $5,000 today) and he laid hands on him, and took him by the throat, saying, Pay me that thou owest. And his fellowservant fell down at his feet, and besought him, saying, Have patience with me, and I will pay thee all. And he would not: but went and cast him into prison, till he should pay the debt."[39]

As I read these passages, the thought came into my mind that I should forgive this twenty-thousand-dollar debt. I recalled many of my own trespasses the Lord had forgiven. Shouldn't I exercise the same compassion and mercy toward my friend? The Lord had forgiven me of debts far greater than twenty thousand dollars, and He provided me with the twenty thousand dollars in the first place.

I called our friend to discuss the situation. He apologized for his dishonesty and for the pain and frustration he had caused our family. He said that he wanted to return our money and that he didn't have the money currently, but if we were patient with him, he would eventually pay us back. I read him the Lord's Prayer and the Lord's parable on forgiveness and told him that the debt was forgiven. He initially resisted the idea, saying, "Twenty thousand dollars is a lot of money; I must pay you back. I cannot take your money." I explained that the money was not mine, but the Lord's. It was not me, but the Lord, who was forgiving the debt. He thanked me, expressing what a help this was to him and his four children. I showed appreciation for his gratitude, but asked that he direct his thanks not to me, but to the Lord.

We are often caught up in the "mine, mine, mine" mentality, allowing greed and selfishness into our hearts. Once we can say "It is the Lord's" instead of "It is mine," we are freed from the attachment to treasures that can be corrupted by rust or taken by thieves.[40]

Defining Our Values

Making the decision before the situation occurs helps us make the correct choices when the pressures of the moment arise. Establishing and committing to a set of values or principles is key to living with integrity. The following four steps may be helpful as you define your own values.

1. Write down the five people you most admire and respect.
2. Next to each name write four or five attributes you most admire about each person. The attributes in your list that appear the most are your core values.
3. Identify five people you don't admire and write down next to their names the attributes that come to mind to describe them. These are attributes you will want to avoid.
4. Review your core values daily. This will help keep you focused on living and achieving your

values and will guard against them being pushed
aside in daily pursuits.

A dear friend and business associate of mine, G. Kent
Mangelson, shared with me the following: "After nearly thirty
years in the financial business and having associated with thousands of wealthy individuals, I have developed a firm philosophy
about people and money. If an individual does not clearly establish personal values and goals before making financial goals, then
wealth and the accumulation thereof will begin to take on a life
of its own. Without clearly established values to keep the individual's direction in focus, money tends to distract the person,
gradually moving him or her away from everything in life that
means the most. Sadly, and all too often, when it is too late to
repair the damage, the person discovers that he or she has lost
those things that meant the most and that all the money in the
world cannot buy or replace that which is gone."

Conclusion

We should each strive to cultivate the proper attitudes toward
the creation and management of earthly riches. The Lord said,
"If you have not been faithful with riches of this world, who will
trust you with true riches?"[41] A faithful steward is one who uses
his or her time, talents, and resources to produce the greatest
amount of good for his or her family, other people, and the
kingdom of God. We must remember the words of the Savior:
"A man's life consisteth not in the abundance of the things which
he possesseth."[42] For "there is one who makes himself rich, yet
has nothing; And one who makes himself poor, yet has great
riches."[43]

CHAPTER 11

THE PARADOX OF GIVING

"One man gives freely, yet gains even more; another with-holds unduly, but comes to poverty. A generous man will prosper; he who refreshes others will himself be refreshed."
—Proverbs 11:24–25, New International Version

"Giving does not cause you to have less, but in fact guarantees that ultimately you will have more."[1] For example, the Old Testament prophet Elijah found a widow who was gathering sticks to prepare her family's final meal, possessing only a handful of flour and a small amount of oil. Elijah said to the widow, "'First make me a little cake of it and bring it to me, and afterward make something for yourself and your son. For thus says the LORD the God of Israel, 'The jar of flour shall not be spent, and the jug of oil shall not be empty, until the day that the LORD sends rain upon the earth.' And she went and did as Elijah said. And she and he and her household ate for many days. The jar of flour was not spent, neither did the jug of oil become empty, according to the word of the LORD that he spoke by Elijah."[2]

The Lord has promised that if we give to Him, He will pour upon us blessings saying, "All who have given up home . . . or land for me will be given a hundred times as much."[3] "If we will share what we have, many people's lives can be blessed, and what we have left will grow at a geometric rate."[4] The Bible declares, "If you give to others, you will be given . . . in return."[5]

We see this principle manifest in our blood. When we give

away our blood, we are able to bless the life of someone else in need, and we are given more blood to replace that which was given away. "Whatever you want more of, give some of it away,"[6] for the Lord replenishes what we give away.

Research on Giving

The following is an excerpt from a lecture[7] given by Arthur C. Brooks, professor at Syracuse University and author of the book *Who Really Cares?*

> I'm an economist, and I also teach in an entrepreneurship department at Syracuse, so I work with successful entrepreneurs all the time. Most of them are exceptionally generous people, and they always tell me the same thing: part of my secret to success is how much I give away. . . . I decided to test this and prove the theory was incorrect, so the next time an entrepreneur told me that part of his or her success was due to their giving, I could say, "I actually tested that, and it's not correct." It turns out the joke was on me. I'm going to show you how wrong I was . . . and how it changed my understanding of charitable giving.
>
> I expected to find that when people got rich they gave more but that when they gave more they didn't necessarily get richer. What I learned . . . is that . . . when people give charitably they also get richer. Imagine you have two families that are exactly the same demographically. Same level of education, number of kids, region of

residence, ages, religion—the only difference is that the first family gives $100 more to charity than the second family. It turns out that first family will earn, on average, $375 more than the nongiving family, and that extra income is attributable to the charitable donation. When I realized this, I thought that was completely wrong. As a matter of fact, I got new data and rewrote my analysis, because I thought I'd done something wrong. The analysis was suggesting that the return on investment to a dollar given to charity is $3.75. That's an incredible investment. So I got new data, and it kept coming up again and again. . . .

[There is a] myth . . . that giving makes us poor, because we give money away. This was the misconception that I had because I was stuck being an economist. I had a mechanistic view of life, but life is not mechanistic. Life is more perfect than that. Giving doesn't make us poor; giving makes us richer.

Tithing

"Honor the LORD by giving him your money and the first part of all your crops. Then you will have more grain and grapes than you will ever need."
—Proverbs 3:9–10, Contemporary English Version

We are to give 10 percent of our annual income as a tithe to the Lord. The book of Genesis tells of Abraham paying tithing to

Melchizedek: "Then Abram gave Melchizedek a tenth of every-thing."[8] Jacob promised the Lord he would pay a tithe, saying, "Of all that you give me I will give you a tenth."[9] Moses received the following command to tithe while on Mount Sinai: "A tithe of everything from the land . . . belongs to the LORD. . . . Thou shalt truly tithe all the increase of thy seed, that the field bringeth forth year by year."[10]

The Lord promises to pour upon us His blessings as we pay tithing, saying, "'Bring the whole tithe into the storehouse, that there may be food in my house. Test me in this,' says the LORD Almighty, 'and see if I will not throw open the floodgates of heaven and pour out so much blessing that you will not have room enough for it. I will prevent pests from devouring your crops . . . ,' says the LORD Almighty."[11]

One of my mentors related to me the following story of a young widow of meager means, with a large family to care for, who went to her pastor to pay her tithing. The pastor said to the widow, "It is not necessary for you to pay tithing; there are those who have an abundance that can support the work of the church." The widow replied to the pastor, "You ought to be ashamed of yourself. Would you deny me a blessing? If I did not pay my tithing, I should expect the Lord to withhold His blessings from me. I pay my tithing, not only because it is a law of God, but because I expect a blessing by doing it. By keeping this and other laws, I expect to prosper, and to be able to provide for my fami-ly." Some argue that they can't afford to pay tithing. Those who understand the blessings that come from paying tithing say, "I can't afford not to pay tithing."

Responsibility of Wealth

> *"We make a living by what we earn—*
> *we make a life by what we give."*
> —Winston Churchill

Since all things belong to the Lord, we are not owners of our wealth, possessions, and property but are stewards for the Lord. "We are the mere trustees of what funds we are temporarily given on this earth."[12] We will be accountable to the Lord for how we manage this stewardship.

Businessman and philanthropist Andrew Carnegie stated, "This, then, is held to be the duty of the man of wealth: First, to set an example of modesty, unostentatious living, shunning display, or extravagance; to provide moderately for the legitimate wants of those dependent upon him; and after doing so to consider all surplus revenues which come to him simply as trust funds, which he is called upon to administer, and strictly bound as a matter of duty to administer in the manner which, in his judgment, is best calculated to produce the most beneficial results for the community."[13]

Thomas Jefferson said, "I deem it the duty of every man to devote a certain portion of his income for charitable purposes; and that it is his further duty to see it so applied as to do the most good of which it is capable."[14] "Charity is the salt which keeps wealth from corruption."[15]

Jon Huntsman, founder of Huntsman Chemical, showed that he understood the stewardship of money when he said, "The Lord has tapped me on the shoulder and said, 'To you, my son, I am entrusting large amounts of money. You determine best how you can redeploy these assets into the community of humankind around you.' . . . Over the years we've spent a lot of money on homelessness and feeding the poor. . . . I received a letter recently. . . . All it said was Homeless Shelter. The letter read: 'Dear Mr. Huntsman. I am warm and dry and out of the cold of last night, and I had a real bed to sleep on. I know you sent some money to keep this shelter, where I am staying, alive. I arose knowing I would shower with warm water and have soap and shampoo and a clean towel to use. Maybe this humble letter does not, or will not mean much within the vastness of the universe, but for this moment in time I just wanted to say with all my heart, thank you. For it means to me a great deal, to this homeless woman a great deal indeed. Thank you.' I've had that letter framed, not because it's important to receive recognition for gifts, but because it's important to know the feeling in the hearts of people when they are down and out and receive help."[16]

Larry Stewart, known as Secret Santa, walked around during the Christmas season anonymously giving small amounts of cash to people in need. His decades of giving started in December 1979. He had just been fired the week before Christmas for the second year in a row and was at a drive-in restaurant feeling sorry for himself when he experienced the joy of giving to others. Larry recalled, "It was cold and this carhop didn't have on a very big jacket, and I thought to myself, 'I think I got it bad. She's out there in this cold making nickels and dimes.' Larry gave the woman twenty dollars. Larry continues, "Suddenly I saw her lips begin to tremble and tears begin to flow down her cheeks. She said, 'Sir, you have no idea what this means to me.'" Larry went to the bank and took out $200 in cash and found people in need to give the money to. He continued this tradition each Christmas for twenty-seven years until his death at the start of 2007. He gave away $1.3 million in hundred-dollar bills during his life. When asked in an interview why he gave so much, he said, "I'm just doing what the Lord is directing me to do. I'm just a pair of hands and feet. He's using me. He's lighted my path. Part of my daily prayer was, 'Lord, let me be a better servant.' I had no idea this is what he had in mind, but I'm happy. I'm so thrilled he is able to use me in this way."

We are to give a percent of our income each year to care for those in need, such as feeding the hungry, clothing the naked, administering to the sick, and "to look after orphans and widows."[17] What percent should we give for these purposes? Jon Huntsman suggests, "There is no set formula, but I would hold that the excess over and above one's guidelines for a comfortable standard of living is a reasonable starting point. . . . We don't need millions of dollars to live comfortably."[18] C. S. Lewis provided this insight: "If our expenditure on comforts, luxuries, amusements, etc., is up to the standard common among those with the same income as our own, we are probably giving away too little. If our charities do not at all pinch or hamper us, I should say they are too small. There ought to be things we should like to do and cannot do because our charitable expenditure excludes them."[19] In the words of St. Augustine, "Find out how much God has given you and from it take what you need: the remainder is needed by others."[20] "God loves a cheerful giver."[21]

Avoid Harmful Help

> *"Charity is injurious unless it helps the recipient*
> *to become independent of it."*
> —John D. Rockefeller, Jr.

There's a story about a wealthy family in which the father had built a large and very successful business from the ground up. As the father approached retirement, he called his son into his office and told his son that he wanted him to eventually take over his company. The son was excited and asked, "When are you going to give it to me?" The father replied, "I am not going to give you anything. You must earn it." The son replied, "How am I supposed to do that?"

The father answered, "First, you must earn ten thousand dollars to purchase a small portion of ownership in the company." As the son left to begin his quest, his mother grabbed him and shoved ten thousand dollars into his hand and told him to give the money to his father. Thrilled by his good fortune, the son ran to his father. His dad was sitting by the fireplace reading a book. The son approached his father and said, "Dad, Dad, here's ten thousand dollars for the business." Without looking up, the father took the money and tossed it into the fire. The son stood, frozen with amazement and watched. As the money burned, the father said, "Come back when you have earned the money."

As he left the room, his mother once again gave him ten thousand dollars and told him to be more convincing in selling his father on the idea that he had actually worked for the money. So the boy scuffed himself up a little, jogged around the block a few times, and then went to find his father again. His father was still sitting in front of the fireplace reading a book. The boy approached his father and said, "It sure is tough earning money. Here's the ten thousand dollars. I really do want to own the business." Once again the father took the ten thousand dollars and tossed it in the fireplace. As the money burned, the son asked, "How did you know I didn't earn the money?" The father replied, "It is easy to lose or spend money that is not your own."

At this point the son realized he wasn't going to get the business unless he actually earned the ten thousand dollars. He wanted the business, so when his mother offered him the money again, he declined her offer. He went out and picked up some odd jobs. His jobs required him to get up early and stay up late, but he worked and worked until he earned ten thousand dollars. Proudly he walked into his father's office and presented him with the money. Like before, his father was sitting by the fire reading a book. And like before, the father took the money and threw it in the fireplace. As the money hit the flames, the son dove to the floor, and stuck his hands into the fire and pulled out the money. The father looked his son in the eyes and said, "I see you really did earn the money this time."

Harmful Help as a Parent

A business owner and church leader shared this experience: "I remember some years ago, a young man and his wife and little children moved to our Arizona community. As we got acquainted with them, he told me of the rigorous youth he had spent as he grew up. He'd had to get up at five and six o'clock in the morning and go out and deliver papers. He'd had to work on the farm, and he'd had to do many things that were still rankling [causing irritation/resentment] in his soul. Then he concluded with this statement: 'My boys are never going to have to do that.' And we saw his boys grow up and you couldn't get them to do anything."

Many parents make the mistake of providing damaging financial assistance to their children. With good intentions, they want to help their children get started in life and offer assistance when a financial need arises. Unfortunately, the result is often opposite to the one desired. Instead of helping children become self-sufficient, the children become dependent. Rather than sparking initiative and discipline, they become idle and indulgent. Instead of being achievement oriented, they become entitlement oriented. Instead of becoming grateful, they become demanding. "Children who always get what they want will want as long as they live."[22] Research has shown that "in general, the more dollars adult children receive [from their parents] the fewer they accumulate, while those who are given fewer dollars accumulate more."[23]

How can we make sure our children grow up with the earning mentality rather than the entitlement mentality? One of the best ways to create an earning mentality in our children is to teach them how to work. However, there is a growing trend of fewer and fewer children working. As parents are providing financially for all their children's needs, many children are no longer working during the summer. In 2007, for the first time on record, the majority of U.S. teenagers were not working or looking for work at the beginning of the summer. Only 49 percent of teens age 16 to 19 were working or looking for work in

June 2007, a steep decline from the 68 percent of teens working or looking for work in June 1978.[24]

There is another trend that I believe is tied to the trend of fewer teens working at jobs. As the number of teens working has gone down, the number of adult children returning to live with their parents has increased. Census figures indicate that millions of so-called empty nesters now find themselves with at least one grown child living at home.[25] The common parental expectation of having an empty nest has given way to the reality of a crowded nest. And a recent survey revealed that 25 percent of the college graduating class expected to live at home after graduating.[26]

To help teach children good work ethics, parents need to look for opportunities for their children to work. I have a seven-year-old son, and he never asks me for money. When there is something he wants, he asks me for jobs he can do to earn the money to purchase the item. He has learned that Mom and Dad will not give him money, but that money has to be earned. I have him help when I do various mailers for my companies. When I come home with the mailers, my son is so excited that he will often yell something along the lines of, "Yes! Dad brought home mailers." It is fun to see a seven-year-old so excited about working and earning money.

Parents should create a financial environment that requires their children to work and earn money by having a job outside of the home to pay for their expenses in their youth and pay their own way through college. I've found that those who had jobs outside of the home while in high school and college have a stronger work ethic than those who did not. Having noticed this trend leads me to believe that teaching a child to work is not simply teaching how to complete tasks or earn money, but it is teaching a way of life. Now as I hire employees, I seek to find those who have a strong work ethic by asking what jobs they had during high school and college. The hardest-working employees I have had are those who had to work their way through high school and college.

If you keep your children from experiencing struggle and responsibility, you will also prevent them from growing. Work ethic, discipline, and initiative cannot be purchased with money, but instead are developed through work, experience, and education. Living off others is a form of bondage—for if you take from a person the responsibility to care for oneself, you also take from that person the opportunity to be free. If you help too much, you make an individual helpless. Do not give your children money; give them education and opportunity. It costs much less and will develop the productive, self-sufficient children you desire.

The Story of the Caterpillar

While starting my first business, I often relied for advice on one of my business partners and mentors who was a multimillionaire. My business was growing, but it struggled to turn a profit. I continued to work hard, but things were getting tighter and tighter financially. I went to my rich partner and asked for a small monthly salary or a loan to help me get by until the business was profitable. He declined to give me any assistance. I was frustrated and said, "You are making millions a year, and I am struggling to stay alive. Please help me." He looked at me, and I could tell he was close to giving in and wanted to help me. "However," he replied, "if I take away your struggle, I will also take away your victory." He then shared the following story.

"There was a young boy who came across a caterpillar hanging in a cocoon. He visited the cocoon several times a day, watching it grow and change and waiting for a butterfly to emerge. After a few days, the young boy began to see the cocoon move and watched as a butterfly struggled to emerge. The boy wanted to help the caterpillar so he ran home and got a pair of scissors. He returned and carefully cut open the cocoon, and out fell a partially developed butterfly. This caterpillar would never fly as a butterfly because it hadn't developed the muscular strength that butterflies gain when struggling to leave the cocoon. The young boy had innocently killed the butterfly he was trying to help." At the time, I didn't find this advice helpful, but today I am grateful to a wise partner and mentor who resisted the temptation to cut open my cocoon.

Conclusion

When you stand before the judgment bar of Christ, He may ask the following: Did you bear the burdens of your neighbor? Did you use your time and money to lift and build others? Did you provide comfort to the sick, lonely, and homeless? Did you use your time and resources to feed the hungry, clothe the naked, and strive to build the kingdom of God? What joy will fill your heart and soul as you answer yes and hear the Lord say to you, "Well done, thou good and faithful servant. . . . Enter into my rest."[27]

CHAPTER 12

THE PARADOX OF FUNDAMENTALS

"Look also at ships: although they are so large and are driven by fierce winds, they are turned by a very small rudder wherever the pilot desires."
—James 3:4, New King James Version

It was with "two small fishes"[1] that thousands of people were fed. It was a small stone David used to slay Goliath.[2] The Savior declares in the New Testament, "The kingdom of God is like . . . a mustard seed, which is the smallest seed you plant in the ground. Yet when planted, it grows and becomes the largest of all garden plants."[3] The Lord is teaching us that it is by small and simple things that great things are brought to pass.

The Bible tells of a leper named Naaman who went to Elisha to be healed, and Elisha told Naaman, "Go and wash in the Jordan seven times, and your flesh shall be restored to you, and you shall be clean."[4] But Naaman rejected the counsel, for he expected a mighty miracle. "Naaman became furious . . . and went away in a rage."[5] Naaman's servant then spoke to him, saying, "If the prophet had told you to do something great, would you not have done it? How much more then, when he says to you, 'Wash, and be clean'?"[6] Naaman then went and washed seven times in the Jordon and was healed.

How often do we make the same mistake that Naaman made and reject the counsel given to us by our pastors because their guidance and direction do not seem great enough to us? Our pastors tell us that Bible study, prayer, and attending church are foundational to our spiritual well-being. We listen to their sermons each week and hear these simple directives and may get upset as did Naaman, saying, "I have heard this all before. Why don't they teach me something new? This is all just so basic. I want to be taught the great doctrines of the gospel." What we may fail to realize is that the basics, the fundamentals of the gospel, are the great doctrines. It is by following these fundamental principles that greatness is brought to pass.

The Bible gives us another example in the book of Numbers: "And the LORD sent fiery serpents among the people, and they bit the people; and much people of Israel died. Therefore the people came to Moses, and said, We have sinned, for we have spoken against the LORD, and against thee; pray unto the LORD, that he take away the serpents from us. And Moses prayed for the people. And the LORD said unto Moses, make thee a fiery serpent, and set it upon a pole: and it shall come to pass, that every one that is bitten, when he looketh upon it, shall live. And Moses made a serpent of brass, and put it upon a pole, and it came to pass, that if a serpent had bitten any man, when he beheld the serpent of brass, he lived."[7]

"The simplicity troubles many people. We expect a more complicated cure, a more elaborate treatment. . . . Manufacture an ointment. Invent a therapeutic lotion. . . . Or at least fight back. Break out the sticks and stones and attack the snakes."[8] The Lord's guidance was not complicated; it was simple and easy to follow, as was the counsel given to Naaman, but because the people looked for some great solution, they failed to look at the brass serpent and perished.

In a sermon delivered in 1914, a pastor shared the power of small and simple acts: "There is no one great thing that we can do to obtain eternal life, and it seems to me that the great lesson to be learned in the world today is to apply in the little acts and duties of life the glorious principles of the Gospel. Let us not think that because some of the things named this afternoon may seem small and trivial, that they are unimportant. Life, after all, is made up of little things. Our life . . . is made up here of little heartbeats. Let that little heart stop beating, and life in this world ceases. The great sun is a mighty force in the universe, but we receive the blessings of his rays because they come to us as little beams, which, taken in the aggregate, fill the whole world with sunlight. The dark night is made pleasant by the glimmer of what seem to be little stars; and so the true Christian life is made up of little Christ-like acts performed this hour, this minute, in the home . . . in the organization, in the town, wherever our life and acts may be cast."

In a sermon titled "The Simple Things," a pastor shared, "As a teenage boy, I began working for a contractor pouring concrete foundations for homes. I learned that concrete was made of a mixture of very simple elements which of themselves were not stable enough for a foundation. But mixed together in proper sequence and proportions, tiny grains of sand, small pebbles, water, and cement powder form a unique substance of unusual strength and durability. For a few hours after the concrete is mixed, it can be poured into any desired form. At first, before it is completely hardened, even a tiny bird hopping across its soft surface will leave an imprint. Later, however, it becomes so firm an elephant could walk over it without leaving any tracks. Just as a few simple elements combined in a proper way form a sturdy foundation for a house, so do the simple teachings of the gospel bond together to make a strong foundation for our lives."

It is the small and simple tasks that produce the great results. "The great truths in life are the simple ones."[9] "Success in life is founded upon attention to the small things rather than to the large things; to the everyday things nearest to us rather than to the things that are remote and uncommon."[10]

Coach John Wooden: Teacher of Fundamentals

"Build your empire on the firm foundation of the fundamentals."
—Lou Holtz

John Wooden was born in the small town of Hall, Indiana in 1910. Just before his twenty-second birthday he began his basketball coaching career at Dayton High School in Kentucky. They finished 6-11 on the year. This was Coach Wooden's only season in which his team had a losing record. After two years at Dayton, he returned to Indiana where he took a job at South Bend Central High School as an English teacher and coach of the basketball, baseball, and tennis teams. Coach left South Bend Central after nine years to serve as a lieutenant in the U.S. Navy during World War II. During his eleven years coaching high school basketball, Coach had an impressive 218-42 record.

Following the war in 1946 Coach took a job at Indiana State University as the athletic director as well as the basketball and baseball coach. Under Coach Wooden, Indiana State won conference championships in 1946 and 1947 and finished as runner-up in the 1947 NAIA tournament.

Shortly after the NAIA tournament, Wooden received a number of coaching offers at larger schools. One of the offers came from UCLA. Coach wrote, "Immediately after accepting the position, I arranged to take a week off from Indiana State to go to Los Angeles to conduct spring basketball practice which was then permitted. On my previous visit I had been all over the campus, visited various administrators and officials, but had not met one of the basketball players. When I went up on the floor for the first time in the spring of 1948 and put them through that first practice, I was very disappointed. I felt my Indiana State team could have named the score against them. I was shattered. Had I known how to abort the agreement in an honorable manner, I would have done so. . . . However, that would be contrary to my creed. I don't believe in quitting, so I resolved to work hard [and] try to develop the talent on hand. . . . After the close of school at Indiana State, I moved my family to Los Angeles, realizing that I had a tremendous job ahead to turn things around. By the time regular practice started, the press had already tabbed us to finish last in the old Pacific Coast Conference. The year before UCLA won 12 and lost 13, and as far as I could determine the three best players . . . were gone. It was like starting from scratch. Almost all of the early practice sessions were devoted to fundamentals, drills, conditioning, and trying to put my philosophy over. Within a few weeks things didn't look quite as dark. . . . We turned things around . . . and won the Southern Division title with a 10 and 2 record. In all, we won 22 and lost 7 for the full season—the most wins any UCLA team had ever compiled in history."[11]

This was the beginning of many accomplishments at UCLA for Coach Wooden; however, it took time to develop a national championship team. John Wooden wrote, "It takes time to create excellence. If it could be done quickly more people would do it."[12] After Coach Wooden's arrival at UCLA, it was sixteen years before they won their first national championship. Over the final twelve years of Wooden's coaching career, UCLA won ten national championships. So what was Coach Wooden's secret to success? Coach taught, "Little things done well is probably the greatest secret to success. . . . If you do enough small things right, big things can happen."[13]

Coach Wooden focused on teaching and practicing the fundamentals. He wrote, "I believe in the basics: attention to, and perfection of, tiny details that might commonly be overlooked. They may seem trivial, perhaps even laughable to those who don't understand, but they aren't. They are fundamental to your progress in basketball, business and life. They are the difference between champions and near-champions. . . . There are little details in everything you do, and if you get away from any one of the little details, you're not teaching the things as a whole. For it is the little things, which, taken together, make the whole. . . . Little things make the big things happen. In fact . . . there are no big things, only a logical accumulation of little things done at a very high standard of performance."[14] Wooden said that there were many who laughed at his repeated focus on and perfection of the small, simple, and basic fundamentals. He wrote, "But I wasn't laughing. I knew very well [they] were the foundation for UCLA's success."[15]

Bill Walton wrote, "Coach Wooden broke it down so the

players could master the fundamentals and therefore could play up to their full potential. That's the thing I remember about UCLA basketball. The practices were more important to me than the games. . . . I remember those simple fundamentals . . . and everything else would take care of itself."[16] "[Gail] Goodrich, who played on UCLA's 30-0 national championship team in 1964, said that he knew he wanted to be a Bruin after he saw his first UCLA practice while still in high school. 'I had never seen anything so organized and precise in my life.'"[17] Carroll Adams said of Coach's practices, "He just drilled you on the strict fundamentals, and when that situation came up in a ball game you handled it because it had become second nature to you."[18] George Stanich recalls that at UCLA, "The practices were the most important thing. Doing the little things."[19]

"From time to time, other coaches or sportswriters would say that UCLA's basketball teams were much too predictable. . . . Everyone knew what they were going to try to do, but they did it so well that no one could stop them anyway! . . . When he was told that others call his offense 'predictable,' Coach simply said, 'I am not a strategy coach. I'm a practice coach.'. . . Coach drilled the fundamentals into his players."[20] John Green, an All-American at UCLA, said, "Coach used the same plays year after year. Everybody knew what we were going to do, but very few could stop us. That's because Coach had us do things over and over again until we did them right."[21]

"Ex-UCLA basketball coach Jim Harrick said, 'John Wooden . . . emphasized that basketball is a very simple game. . . . You learn to win games from 3:00 to 5:30 every day at practice, certainly not the night of the game. Coach agrees: 'What I taught was as simple as one, two, three.'"[22]

In 1975, during Coach Wooden's final season, Myron

Finkbeiner recalls watching the Bruins practice during the Final Four. "It was amazing to watch them, because Coach put them through the same drills he had used on the first day of practice at the beginning of the season. They ran through simple passing drills, pivoting moves, blocking-out routines. John Wooden was redoing the fundamentals all over again."[23] UCLA went on to win its tenth national championship. After forty years of coaching, Wooden continued to focus on, teach, and practice the simple fundamentals, for they were the source of his success. Coach lived his words: "Do the basics right, and do as well as you can with what God gave you, and you will be surprised at how far you can get in life. . . . Little things make big things happen."[24]

Conclusion

After having built a business from idea to a million dollars a month in five years, I was often asked what the secret to my success was. I would reply that the key to my success was prayer and meditation at the beginning of each day to seek guidance and help from the Lord in my efforts. I remember on one occasion after I provided this response, the inquirer got mad and said something along the lines of, "If you don't want to tell me your secret, just say so," and then walked off. So often we look for a magic secret or great technique that will produce great returns and results. Those seeking the big secret soon discover that the secret is to continually live and apply basic, simple fundamentals.

Each year at an annual youth retreat I deliver a speech titled "Live Your Dreams: Five Steps to Goal Achievement." One of the students who returned the following year for the retreat came up to me to share his experience with goal setting over the last year. He told me of all the wonderful things he accomplished. His parents, teachers, and classmates begin to ask what had changed and what made it possible for him to accomplish so much over the past year. He responded to their questions by saying he began writing down his goals and working to achieve them. He said that most of those who inquired were very surprised by his simple answer. Goal setting is a simple, fundamental process that produces a dramatic increase in what you can accomplish, yet 97 percent of people do not do it. Studies have found that only 3 percent of Americans have written goals.

College coaching great Abe Lemons once said, "I think people try to read something complicated into John Wooden's life, but I think it's so simple that people can't believe it."[25] Naaman thought Elisha's counsel to wash in the Jordan was too simple to work, and the people bitten by poisonous snakes thought a cure by looking at a brass snake was too simple. We have a natural tendency to see the simple solutions and guidelines that God has given us and think, "It can't be that simple," and then try to complicate them or simply neglect to do these simple basics. We would do well to remember that the small things are the great things and that learning to do the small things well will eventually produce greatness within us. For "the kingdom of God is like . . . a mustard seed, which is the smallest seed you plant in the ground. Yet when planted, it grows and becomes the largest of all garden plants."[26]

CONCLUSION

It is through the application of the Lord's paradoxical advice that we truly come to know the truth. As the apostle John taught, "If any man will do His will, he shall know of the doctrine, whether it be of God, or whether I speak of myself."[1]

The Paradox of Faith
"He that findeth his life shall lose it: and he that loseth his life for my sake shall find it."
—Matthew 10:39, King James Version

The Paradox of Grace
"And he [Christ] said unto me [Paul], My grace is sufficient for thee: for my strength is made perfect in weakness. Most gladly therefore will I rather glory in my infirmities, that the power of Christ may rest upon me . . . for when I am weak, then am I strong."
—2 Corinthians 12:9–10, King James Version

The Paradox of Performance
"But many that are first shall be last; and the last shall be first."
—Matthew 19:30, King James Version

The Paradox of Leadership
"He that is greatest among you shall be your servant."
—Matthew 23:11, King James Version

The Paradox of Wisdom
"Professing themselves to be wise, they became fools. . . . Let him become a fool, that he may be wise."
—Romans 1:22; 1 Corinthians 3:18, King James Version

The Paradox of Receiving

*"For whosoever receiveth, to him shall be given, and he shall have
more abundance; but whosoever continueth not to receive, from
him shall be taken away even that he hath."*

—Matthew 13:10–11, Inspired Version

The Paradox of Pain

"Consider it pure joy . . . whenever you face trials of many kinds."

—James 1:2, New International Version

The Paradox of Choice

*"They answered him [Jesus], We . . . were never in bondage to
any man: how sayest thou, Ye shall be made free? Jesus
answered them, Verily, verily, I say unto you, Whosoever
committeth sin is the servant of sin."*

—John 8:33–34, King James Version

The Paradox of Forgiveness

*"Ye have heard that it hath been said, An eye for an eye, and a
tooth for a tooth: But I say unto you, That ye resist not evil: but
whosoever shall smite thee on thy right cheek, turn to him the other
also. And if any man will sue thee at the law, and take away thy
coat, let him have thy cloak also."*

—Matthew 5:38–40, King James Version

The Paradox of Wealth

*"There is one who makes himself rich, yet has nothing;
And one who makes himself poor, yet has great riches."*

—Proverbs 13:7, New King James Version

The Paradox of Giving

"One man gives freely, yet gains even more; another withholds unduly, but comes to poverty. A generous man will prosper; he who refreshes others will himself be refreshed."

—Proverbs 11:24–25, New International Version

The Paradox of Fundamentals

"Look also at ships: although they are so large and are driven by fierce winds, they are turned by a very small rudder wherever the pilot desires."

—James 3:4, New King James Version

It is my prayer and hope that this book has been enjoyable and helpful to you. I would love to hear from you. Please tell me what you enjoyed about the book and how it has impacted your life.

Cameron C. Taylor
428 E. Thunderbird Road #504
Phoenix, AZ 85022
CTaylor@DoesYourBagHaveHoles.org

My Witness of Christ

True success and happiness are found in the teaching of the Master Jesus Christ. Christ is the light and life of the world and the foundation upon which if men and women will build they shall never fall. I do share my witness that I know that we are each children of a loving Heavenly Father who knows each of us personally and intimately. I do testify that Jesus Christ is the Son of God. The accounts of His life and ministry recorded in the New Testament are true. Jesus healed the sick, caused the lame to walk, gave sight unto the blind, raised the dead, comforted and lifted the weak, and embraced and forgave the sinner. He lived a perfect life, and He did take upon Himself the sins of the world. He is our Savior and Redeemer who is full of grace and truth. He was crucified; His body was laid inside a tomb, and on the third day following His death on the cross He did rise from the dead. He is the resurrection and the life. I do share my witness that Jesus Christ lives. I know that He lives. I know that Jesus Christ lives. Christ is the path that leads to happiness in this life and eternal life in the world to come. May the grace of our Lord and Master Jesus Christ be with you all. Amen.

Cameron C. Taylor

ENDNOTES

Preface

1 Paul Schatzkin, *The Boy Who Invented Television* (Silver Spring, MD: Teamcom Books, 2002), 249.

Chapter 1

1 Matthew 10:39, King James Version.
2 St. Augustine, as quoted in James Nichols, *The Works of James Arminius, D.D.* Vol. 1 (Auburn and Buffalo, NY: Derby, Miller and Orton, 1853), 526.
3 C. S. Lewis, *Mere Christianity* (London: Harper Collins, 1996), 191.
4 Ibid., 190–91.
5 Matthew 14:25–31, King James Version.
6 Matthew 14:29, King James Version.
7 Mark 9:23, King James Version.
8 Acts 6:8, King James Version.
9 Matthew 17:20, King James Version.

Chapter 2

1 Stanley Voke, *Personal Revival* (Waynesboro, GA: OM Literature), 24.
2 Luke 18:10–14, King James Version.
3 Luke 22:44, King James Version.
4 Romans 5:8–21, King James Version.
5 Luke 18:13, King James Version.
6 Matthew 11:28–30, King James Version.
7 Stephen E. Robinson, *Believing Christ* (Salt Lake City: Deseret Book, 1992), 24–25.
8 John 3:3, King James Version.
9 Galatians 5:17, King James Version.
10 Romans 7:14, 15, 19, 24, King James Version.
11 Romans 4:5.
12 Mark 2:17, King James Version.
13 Abraham Booth, *By God's Grace Alone* (London: Grace Publication Trust, 1983), 48–49.
14 C. S. Lewis, *Mere Christianity* (New York: Touchstone, 1996), 131.
15 James 2:18, King James Version.
16 Romans 6:15, King James Version.
17 Matthew 5:48, King James Version.
18 Colossians 3:10, New Century Version.
19 2 Corinthians 3:18, The Message.
20 Ephesians 4:13, Today's English Version.

Chapter 3

1 Matthew 19:30, King James Version.
2 Matthew 5:48, King James Version.
3 David Noel Freedman, *The Anchor Bible Dictionary*, vol. 6 (New York: Doubleday, 1992), 907. Walter A. Elwell, *Baker Encyclopedia of the Bible*, vol. 1 (Grand Rapids: Baker Book House, 1988), 491. During the time of the New Testament, a talent was approximately 750 ounces of silver. A pence was approximately one-eighth of an ounce of silver. Thus, one talent equaled 6,000 pence (750 divided by .125). One pence was the day wage of a laborer. To calculate the 2010 dollar value equivalents, I estimated the wage of a 2010 laborer at $50 per day and multiplied that by the number of pence. Thus, one talent in the New Testament is equal to $300,000 in 2010 in U.S. currency (6,000 multiplied by $50).
4 Matthew 25:21, King James Version.

5 Matthew 25:26–27, 30, New International Version.
6 Revelation 3:17, King James Version.
7 Revelation 3:17, New International Version.
8 Revelation 3:16, English Standard Version.
9 Mark 11:13, New King James Version.
10 Isaiah 28:13, King James Version.
11 Matthew 13:12, Inspired Version.
12 Jeremiah 8:13, New International Version.
13 Edwin A. Locke, *The Essence of Leadership* (New York: Lexington Books, 1991), 79.
14 Nehemiah 9:17, King James Version.
15 Isaiah 1:18, King James Version; Jeremiah 31:34, King James Version.
16 1 John 1:7–9, King James Version.
17 Matthew 9:2, King James Version.

Chapter 4

1 Bob Briner and Ray Pritchard, *Leadership Lessons of Jesus* (New York: Gramercy, 2001), 294–296.
2 Mark 9:33–35, King James Version.
3 Briner and Pritchard, *Leadership Lessons of Jesus*, 293–94.
4 Matthew 23:11, King James Version.
5 Pat Williams and Jim Denney, *How to Be Like Jesus* (Deerfield Beach, FL: Faith Communications, 2003), 372–73.
6 Mark 1:40–42, King James Version.
7 John Stevens Cabot Abbott, *The History of Napoleon Bonaparte*, vol. 1 (New York: Harper & Brothers, 1883), 246.
8 Matthew 20:25–28, King James Version.
9 Williams and Denney, *How to Be Like Jesus*, 378–79.
10 Jared Sparks, *The Life of Benjamin Franklin* (Boston: Whittemore, Niles and Hall, n.d.), 408.
11 Jared Sparks, *The Writings of George Washington*, vol. 4 (Boston: Ferdinand Andrews, 1838), 37–38.
12 *United States Department of Veteran Affairs*, http://www1.va.gov/opa/fact/amwars.asp (accessed June 30, 2008).
13 Edwin Burrows, *Forgotten Patriots: The Untold Story of American Prisoners During the Revolutionary War* (New York: Basic Books, 2008).
14 W. T. R. Saffell, *Records of the Revolutionary War* (Baltimore: Charles C. Saffell, 1894), 304–6.
15 Long Island Genealogy, "Martyrdom of Thirteen Thousand American Patriots aboard the Monstrous Jersey and Other British Prison Ships in New York Harbor," http://www.longislandgenealogy.com/prison.html (accessed November 7, 2008).
16 Saffell, *Records of the Revolutionary War*, 307.
17 James Madison, *The Papers of James Madison*, vol. 2 (Washington, DC: Langtree & O'Sullivan, 1840), 718–19.
18 Matthew 23:11, King James Version.
19 John Marshall, *The Life of George Washington*, vol. 1 (Philadelphia: Crissy & Markley and Thomas, Cowperthwait and Co., 1848), 85.
20 James Baird McClure, *Abraham Lincoln's Stories and Speeches* (Chicago: Rhodes & McClure, 1906), 22.
21 Ibid., 32.
22 Arthur C. Brooks, "The Privilege of Giving," *Marriott Alumni Magazine*, Winter 2008, 20.
23 McClure, *Abraham Lincoln's Stories and Speeches*, 45.
24 John G. Nicolay and John Hay, *Abraham Lincoln, Complete Works*, vol. 1 (New York: Century Co., 1907), 65, 151, 152, 153, 154, 156, 158, 159, 210, 216, 247, 273, 276, 277, 520, 533, 638, 644, 657, 659, 663, 664, 666, 667, 670, 671, 672.

25 McClure, *Abraham Lincoln's Stories and Speeches*, 157.

26 Ibid., 185–86.

27 Ida Minerva Tarbell, *The Life of Abraham Lincoln*, vol. 2 (New York: Macmillan Company, 1917), 125.

28 McClure, *Abraham Lincoln's Stories and Speeches*, 179–80.

29 B. F. Morris, *Memorial Record of the Nation's Tribute to Abraham Lincoln* (Washington, DC: W. H. & O. H. Morrison, 1865), 267.

30 Laurie Beth Jones, *Jesus, CEO* (New York: Hyperion, 1995), 148.

Chapter 5

1   Proverbs 3:5–6, King James Version.

2   Numbers 22:22–34, Contemporary English Version.

3   Proverbs 27:6, Contemporary English Version.

4   Hebrews 12:10, New International Version.

5   Hebrews 12:6, English Standard Version.

6   Proverbs 3:11, King James Version.

7   Blain Lee, *The Power Principle* (New York: Simon & Schuster, 1997), 132.

8   B. J. Losing, *Signers of the Declaration of Independence* (New York: George F. Colledge & Brother, 1848), 167.

9   Proverbs 19:20, New International Version.

Chapter 6

1   David Noel Freedman, *The Anchor Bible Dictionary*, vol. 6 (New York: Doubleday, 1992), 907. Walter A. Elwell, *Baker Encyclopedia of the Bible*, vol. 1 (Grand Rapids: Baker Book House, 1988), 491. See chap. 3, note 3.

2   Matthew 25:21, King James Version.

3   Matthew 25:26, King James Version.

4   Matthew 25:29, King James Version.

5   John 10:10, King James Version.

6   James 4:2, King James Version.

7   Romans 8:26, King James Version.

8   James 4:3.

9   Matthew 17:14–21, King James Version.

10 Matthew 7:9–11, King James Version.

11 Matthew 7:7, King James Version.

Chapter 7

1   Genesis 3:19, New International Version.

2   Genesis 3:17, King James Version.

3   2 Corinthians 8:2, King James Version.

4   1 Peter 1:7, King James Version.

5   1 Peter 4:12–13, King James Version.

6   Isaiah 30:20, King James Version.

7   John 16:33, King James Version.

8   Job 1:1, King James Version.

9   Job 22:5.

10 John 9:1–3, King James Version.

11 Harold S. Kushner, *When Bad Things Happen to Good People* (New York: Avon Books, 1981), 58.

12 Matthew 5:45, Contemporary English Version.

13 C. S. Lewis, *Mere Christianity* (New York: Simon & Schuster, 1996), 176.

14 C. S. Lewis, *The Problem of Pain* (New York: HarperCollins, 2001), 25.

15 John 15:2, New King James Version.

16 Lewis, *Mere Christianity*, 176.

17 Philippians 1:6, New Century Version.

18 Hebrews 12:10, New International Version.

19 Hebrews 12:6, English Standard Version.

20 Lewis, *Problem of Pain*, 93.

21 Tony Dungy and Nathan Whitaker, *Quiet Strength* (Carol Stream, IL: Tyndale House, 2008), 181–82.

22 2 Corinthians 11:24–26, Contemporary English Version.

23 Abraham Lincoln, Address at a Sanitary Fair, Baltimore, Maryland, April 18, 1864.

24 Matthew 5:10–11, Contemporary English Version.

25 Matthew 5:12, King James Version.

26 John McCain, *Why Courage Matters* (New York: Random House, 2004), 91.

27 Brother Lawrence, *Brother Lawrence: The Practice of the Presence of God the Best Rule of a Holy Life, Being Conversations and Letters of Nicholas Herman of Lorraine* (New York: Fleming H. Revell, 1895), 43.

28 Kushner, *When Bad Things Happen to Good People*, 8–9.

29 Matthew 5:12.

30 Hyrum W. Smith, *Pain Is Inevitable, Misery Is Optional* (Salt Lake City: Deseret Book, 2004), 8.

31 McCain, *Why Courage Matters*, 206.

32 Matthew 11:28–30, King James Version.

33 2 Chronicles 32:7, New International Version.

34 2 Timothy 4:7–8, King James Version.

35 Matthew 25:21, King James Version.

Chapter 8

1 John 8:34, New King James Version.

2 Deuteronomy 11:26–28, King James Version.

3 The story from the beginning to the conversation at a chamber of commerce meeting is an account from my memory of an experience I had teaching at a prison. The conversation at the chamber of commerce meeting is based on a story from the life of one of my mentors. I felt the principles taught by the story from my mentor could best be told in the context of the prison encounter. Thus, the encounter with the prisoner at a chamber of commerce meeting is fictional but is based on a true story.

Chapter 9

1 Matthew 26:47–49.

2 Matthew 26:50.

3 Matthew 26:60.

4 Matthew 26:67, King James Version.

5 Matthew 26:67, New King James Version.

6 Matthew 26:67, New American Standard Bible.

7 Matthew 27:2, Contemporary English Version.

8 Matthew 27:28, Contemporary English Version.

9 Mathew 27:26.

10 Matthew 27:29, King James Version.

11 Ibid.

12 Matthew 27:30, King James Version.

13 John 19:17.
14 John 19:18.
15 Luke 23:24, King James Version.
16 Matthew 5:43–44, King James Version.
17 Eknath Easwaran, *Gandhi the Man* (Petaluma, CA: Nilgiri Press, 1997), 47.
18 Buddha, cited in Sue Patton Thoele, *Growing Hope* (York Beach, ME: Red Wheel/Weiser, 2004), 148.
19 Gandhi quoted in Anand Sharma, *Gandhian Way: Peace, Non-violence, and Empowerment* (Darya Ganj, New Delhi, India: Academic Foundation, 2007), 25.
20 Easwaran, *Gandhi the Man*, 49, 56.
21 M. V. Vamath, *Gandhi, A Spiritual Journey* (Mumbai, India: Indus Source Books, 2007), 77.
22 Jafar Mahmud, *Mahatma Gandhi* (New Delhi: A. P. H. Publishing, 2004), 25.
23 George G. Ritchie with Elizabeth Sherrill, *Return from Tomorrow* (Grand Rapids: Fleming H. Revell, 1978), 114–16.
24 2 Kings 5:10, New King James Version.
25 2 Kings 5:11, New King James Version.
26 2 Kings 5:12, New King James Version.
27 2 Kings 5:13, New King James Version.
28 Adolf Rosenberg, *Leonardo da Vinci* (Bielfeld and Leipzig: Velhagen & Klasing, 1903), 68–70; James Hastings, *The Expository Times*, vol. 19 (Edinburgh: T. & T. Clark, 1908), 427.

Chapter 10

1   Robert C. Gay, *Business with Integrity* (Provo, UT: Brigham Young University Press, 2005), 49.
2   Proverbs 13:7, New King James Version.
3   C. S. Lewis, *Mere Christianity* (New York: Simon & Schuster, 1996), 166.
4   Matthew 18:18–25, King James Version.
5   Luke 18:26, King James Version.
6   Mark 10:24, King James Version, emphasis added.
7   Luke 6:20, King James Version.
8   1 Timothy 6:17, King James Version.
9   Deuteronomy 8:18, King James Version.
10 Genesis 13:2, King James Version.
11 Genesis 26:13–14, English Standard Version.
12 Matthew 27:57, King James Version.
13 Matthew 6:33, King James Version.
14 Luke 14:26, King James Version.
15 Herb Miller, *Money Is Everything* (Nashville: Discipleship Resources, 1994), 23.
16 1 Timothy 6:10, King James Version, emphasis added.
17 David Van Biema and Jeff Chu, "Does God Want You To Be Rich?" *Time*, September 10, 2006.
18 Ephesians 4:6, New Century Version.
19 Genesis 3:19, New King James Version.
20 1 Timothy 5:8, King James Version.
21 Brother Lawrence, *Brother Lawrence: The Practice of the Presence of God the Best Rule of a Holy Life, Being Conversations and Letters of Nicholas Herman of Lorraine* (New York: Fleming H. Revell, 1895), 19, 11.
22 Ibid., 20, 13.
23 Sam Walton, *Sam Walton* (New York: Doubleday, 1992), 252–53.
24 Rick Warren, *The Purpose-Driven Life* (Grand Rapids: Zondervan, 2002), 88.
25 Colossians 3:23, New American Standard Bible.
26 Luke 12:15, New International Version.
27 Isaiah 56:11, King James Version.

28 Ecclesiastes 5:10, New International Version.
29 Luke 12:16–20, New International Version.
30 Luke 16:19–23, New International Version.
31 Malachi 3:5, New King James Version.
32 1 Timothy 3:3, 8; Titus 1:7, 11; 1 Peter 5:2, King James Version.
33 Matthew 16:26, King James Version.
34 Joshua 1:8, New International Version.
35 George Q. Cannon, *Gospel Truth: Discourses and Writings of George Q. Cannon*, selected, arranged, and ed. Jerreld L. Newquist (Salt Lake City: Deseret Book, 1987), 525.
36 Matthew 6:11, King James Version.
37 Matthew 6:12, 14–15, King James Version.
38 David Noel Freedman, *The Anchor Bible Dictionary*, vol. 6 (New York: Doubleday, 1992), 907. Walter A. Elwell, *Baker Encyclopedia of the Bible*, vol. 1 (Grand Rapids: Baker Book House, 1988), 491. See chap. 3, note 3.
39 Matthew 18:28–30, King James Version.
40 Matthew 6:19.
41 Luke 16:10–11, New Life Version.
42 Luke 12:15, King James Version.
43 Proverbs 13:7, New King James Version.

Chapter 11

1 Mark Victor Hansen, *The Miracle of Tithing* (Newport Beach, CA: Mark Victor Hansen & Associates, 2002), 49.
2 1 Kings 17:13–16, English Standard Version.
3 Matthew 19:29, Contemporary English Version.
4 Hyrum Smith, *The 10 Natural Laws of Successful Time and Life Management* (New York: Warner Books, 1994), 203.
5 Luke 6:38, Contemporary English Version.
6 Hansen, *Miracle of Tithing*, 9.
7 Arthur C. Brooks, "The Privilege of Giving," *Marriott Alumni Magazine*, Winter 2008, 16–21.
8 Genesis 14:20, Contemporary English Version.
9 Genesis 28:22, New International Version.
10 Leviticus 27:30, New International Version; Deuteronomy 14:22, King James Version.
11 Malachi 3:10–11, New International Version.
12 Andrew Carnegie quoted in Jon M. Huntsman, *Winners Never Cheat* (Upper Saddle River, NJ: Wharton School Publishing, 2005), 151.
13 Andrew Carnegie, *The Gospel of Wealth and Other Timely Essays* (New York: The Century Co., 1901), 15.
14 Thomas Jefferson, *The Writings of Thomas Jefferson*, vol. 11 (Washington, DC: Thomas Jefferson Memorial Association, 1903), 92–93.
15 Lady Katie Magnus, *Jewish Portraits* (London: T. Fisher Unwin, 1888), 151.
16 Jon M. Huntsman Sr., *Business with Integrity* (Provo, UT: Brigham Young University Press, 2005), 98, 101–2.
17 James 1:27, New International Version.
18 Hunstman, *Winners Never Cheat*, 167.
19 C. S. Lewis, *Mere Christianity*, (New York: Simon & Schuster, 1996), 82.
20 St. Augustine, quoted in Hunstman, *Winners Never Cheat*, 151.
21 Corinthians 9:7, New King James Version.
22 Fred G. Gosman, *Spoiled Rotten* (New York: Villard, 1992), 32.
23 Thomas J. Stanley and William D. Danko, *The Millionaire Next Door* (New York: Simon & Schuster, 1996), 142–43.

24 Barbara Hagenbaugh, "More Than Half of Teens Forgo Summer Jobs," *USA Today*, July 9, 2007.

25 Roberta Rand, "When Adult Children Move Back Home," http://www.focusonthefamily.com/midlife/adult_children/the_empty_nest_syndrome/when _adult_children_move_back_home.aspx

26 Sheila J. Curran, "The Adult-Child Comes Home," *Duke University News*, July 21, 2006.

27 Matthew 25:21, King James Version; Psalms 95:11, King James Version.

Chapter 12

1 John 6:9, King James Version.

2 1 Samuel 17:40–49.

3 Mark 4:30-32, New International Version.

4 2 Kings 5:10, New King James Version.

5 2 Kings 5:11–12, New King James Version.

6 2 Kings 5:13, New King James Version.

7 Numbers 21:6–9, King James Version.

8 Max Lucado with Tricia Goyer, *3:16: The Numbers of Hope* (Nashville: Thomas Nelson, 2007), 96.

9 Dr. Steve Franklin quoted in Pat Williams with David Winbish, *How to Be Like Coach Wooden* (Deerfield Beach, FL: Health Communications, 2006), 210.

10 Booker T. Washington quoted in Jim Canterucci, *Personal Brilliance* (New York: AMACOM, 2005), 149.

11 John Wooden with Jack Tobin, *They Call Me Coach* (New York: McGraw-Hill Companies, 2004), 76–78.

12 John Wooden with Steve Jamison, *Wooden: A Lifetime of Observations and Reflections On and Off the Court* (New York: McGraw-Hill, 1997), 191.

13 John Wooden with Steve Jamison, *My Personal Best* (New York: McGraw-Hill, 2004), 106.

14 Wooden, *Wooden*, 60; Swen Nater and Ronald Gallimore, *You Haven't Taught until They Have Learned: John Wooden's Teaching Principles and Practices* (Morgantown, WV: Fitness Information Technology, 2005), 91; John Wooden and Steve Jamison, *Wooden on Leadership* (New York: McGraw-Hill, 2005), 135.

15 Wooden and Jamison, *Wooden on Leadership*, 136.

16 Williams, *How to Be Like Coach Wooden*, 72

17 Ibid., 80.

18 Ibid., 154.

19 Ibid., 195.

20 Ibid., 72.

21 Ibid., 151.

22 Ibid., 73.

23 Ibid., 153–54.

24 Neville L. Johnson, *The John Wooden Pyramid of Success* (Los Angeles: Cool Titles, 2003), 331, 191.

25 Williams, *How to Be Like Coach Wooden*, 205.

26 Mark 4:30–32, New International Version.

Conclusion

1 John 7:17, King James Version.

ILLUSTRATION CREDITS

About the Author

Cameron C. Taylor is the author of several books, including *Does Your Bag Have Holes? 24 Truths That Lead to Financial and Spiritual Freedom, Twelve Paradoxes of the Gospel, 8 Attributes of Great Achievers,* and *The Statement of Excellence Workbook.* Cameron has served in an overseas missionary ministry and currently serves as a volunteer pastor in his local congregation. He is the founder and president of multiple organizations, including the Does Your Bag Have Holes? Foundation. Cameron and his wife Paula have three children.

About the Does Your Bag Have Holes? Foundation™

All author proceeds from this book go to the Does Your Bag Have Holes? Foundation. The foundation is a nonprofit educational charity. Its mission is to inspire the world to learn and live the principles of freedom. The foundation seeks to achieve this mission through publishing books, holding seminars, and providing speakers to churches, businesses, universities, associations, and other organizations. All revenue and donations are used to further the foundation's mission and for other humanitarian efforts.

Does Your Bag Have Holes? Foundation
428 E. Thunderbird Road #504, Phoenix, AZ 85022
Phone: 1-877-664-6537 • Fax: 1-480-393-4432
Service@DoesYourBagHaveHoles.org
www.DoesYourBagHaveHoles.org

OTHER BOOKS BY CAMERON C. TAYLOR

DOES YOUR BAG HAVE HOLES?
24 Truths That Lead to Financial and Spiritual Freedom
ISBN-13: 978-0-979686-10-8, 320 pages with abridged audio book on CD

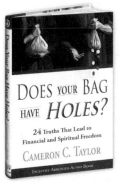

"*Does Your Bag Have Holes?* looks at many of the scriptural principles that lead to real success and true happiness. This valuable resource gives clarity to the truths of a Christian worldview and dispels many of the deceptions of our postmodern culture. It is a must-read for all Christians!"

Finn Laursen, Executive Director
Christian Educators Association International

8 ATTRIBUTES OF GREAT ACHIEVERS
ISBN-13: 978-1-933715-89-6, 160 pages

8 Attributes of Great Achievers is filled with inspiring stories from the lives of great achievers past and present including Christopher Columbus, George Washington, Benjamin Franklin, the Wright Brothers, Abraham Lincoln, Gandhi, Winston Churchill, Walt Disney, Warren Buffett, and others.

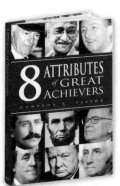

From this book, you will learn:
- How Winston Churchill's optimism enabled England to withstand the attacks of Hitler and eventually win the war.
- How Walt Disney used the power of goals to create (Snow White, Disneyland, etc.) and make his dreams come true.

INVITE CAMERON C. TAYLOR TO SPEAK

Cameron C. Taylor has presented to organizations all across the country. He would be honored to be a part of one of your meetings. Below are some of his presentations, which he can tailor and adapt to fit your needs.

Title: Paradoxes of the Gospel
Summary: Based on the book *12 Paradoxes of the Gospel*. Cameron can speak on one, a few, or all twelve of the gospel paradoxes. In the presentation, he shares inspiring stories, parables, and scriptures.

Title: Powerful Truths of the Bible
Summary: In his book *Does Your Bag Have Holes?* Cameron shares twenty-four biblical truths. He can talk on one, a few, or all twenty-four of the biblical truths. This engaging and entertaining seminar presents parables, metaphors, and inspiring real-life stories that have been developed through years of research.

Title: Live Your Dreams: 5 Steps to Inspired Goal Achievement
Summary: From this presentation you will learn:
- Steps to discover your God-given missions.
- Steps to achieve your inspired goals.
- Powerful stories, analogies, and scriptures.

Other Topics:
Divine-Centered Leadership
8 Attributes of Great Achievers
How to Succeed with People
The Statement of Excellence Workshop

For more information or to schedule Cameron C. Taylor to speak, call 1-877-664-6537 or send an email to Speaker@DoesYourBagHaveHoles.org

.